GCSE
Business and Communication Systems

Teacher Support Pack

Paula Miles

Published in 2003 by:
Nelson Thornes Ltd
Delta Place
27 Bath Road
CHELTENHAM
GL53 7TH
United Kingdom

03 04 05 06 07 / 10 9 8 7 6 5 4 3 2 1

A catalogue record for this book is available from the British Library

ISBN 0 7487 7099 2

Illustrations by Oxford Designers and Illustrators, additional illustrations by IFA Design Ltd, Plympton, Plymouth
Page make-up by IFA Design Ltd, Plympton, Plymouth

Printed in Great Britain by Antony Rowe

Contents

Composition

Assignments

Case Studies

Contents

The author and publishers are grateful to the following for permission to reproduce material:

- Amazon – Amazon.co.uk is a trademark of Amazon.com, Inc. in the US and/or other countries.
- British Waterways.
- Chelsea Building Society.
- Hind and Hart Narrowboat Hotels.
- National Westminster Bank.
- Premier Nanny and Au Pair Agency.
- Tesco Stores Ltd.
- The Assessment and Qualifications Alliance.
- William Grey Power Tools.

Aims and objectives of business organisations

Business aims include:

- Increasing sales.
- Gaining market share.
- Generating profits.
- Maintaining a positive cash flow.

TASK

Which of these aims would you recommend the following businesses to focus on? (A business can have more than one aim.)

Pendleton Pottery

Carrie Pendleton has been trading for three years as a sole trader. She makes and sells ceramic items. Although she realises that mugs, bowls and plates sell well, she is more interested in being commissioned to make ceramic sculptures for display. This approach means that Carrie is finding it difficult to keep her business running. She rents her studio and lives with her parents. Last week's clay order was not delivered as she had not paid the previous month's bill. The studio rent is due in a fortnight and Carrie had relied on finishing, and being paid for, a sculpture for a local hotel. She has run out of clay and the hotel owner is threatening to cancel the order because it has taken longer to complete than Carrie said it would.

Sewell Motors

Kier Sewell took over his uncle's repair garage nine years ago. Kier completed his apprenticeship as a motor mechanic with his uncle. It was clear that Kier had a good understanding of running a business, as well as being a good mechanic, so it was arranged that he would buy the business when his uncle retired.

Kier's business deals mainly with cars over three years old. He has acquired a reputation for explaining clearly what is wrong with a vehicle and giving a realistic estimate of the repair costs. Consequently, he has built up a loyal clientele consisting mainly of car owners who admit they do not understand what goes on under the bonnet and are happy to trust Kier's judgement.

Kier employs two other mechanics and has an apprentice who is just starting his final year of training.

A property adjacent to the garage has unexpectedly come up for sale. It is a small bungalow with a large garden and a variety of storage sheds and garages. It is being used by a small classic-car restoration business. Kier has spoken to a planning officer at the local council and knows that he could expand his business onto these premises and use part of the bungalow as an office and part as his home. His bank is willing to lend him the money he needs, but Kier is anxious – is it worth the risk?

Theresa's Guest House

Theresa O'Neill inherited her parents' house last year. She decided to run it as a guest house as it has six bedrooms and is too large for her and her husband. She had always wanted to run a guest house but had dreamed of a cottage by the sea, not a large Victorian house in a busy town!

At first, Theresa was unsure where her guests would come from – the town is not a holiday resort. However, with some guidance from her business bank manager, she soon found her customers. The town is situated five miles from a large university, and Theresa's house is on the bus route. Some of her customers are students who could not get university accommodation. They stay with her until the accommodation office find lodgings for them. Parents visiting their children stay with Theresa, and she has built up a good reputation with the university

Aims and objectives of business organisations

T A S K

accommodation office who now recommend her. Other customers are business representatives who, when they are working in the area, prefer to stay at her guest house rather than at a hotel. Another source of customers is the local headquarters of a major bank. Staff are sent to the bank on training courses and accommodation is arranged at the guest house. Theresa also has a long-term guest, Mr Hooper, who has been relocated to the area from London. Mrs Hooper has stayed in London whilst their children finish school, and the family intend to move to the area in four or five years' time. Mr Hooper spends the weekends at home with his family.

Perfect Private Tutors

Perfect Private Tutors is an agency owned and run by Lucy and Mike Fowler. They started it when they were unable to find a tutor for their daughter. The agency now employs teachers (both those who are retired and those working part time) who travel to the clients' homes to tutor in a variety of subjects.

Parents contact the agency and explain what help they need. Lucy or Mike then contact a suitable teacher and ask if they can help. The parents pay the agency £25 per hour or £40 for two hours' tutoring. The teacher is paid by the agency at a rate of £15 per hour. There are 85 teachers on the agency's books.

Stakeholders

Stakeholders are individuals, groups or suppliers who are involved in the business in some way. They may either influence the business or be affected by it. Think of your school, for example. Local shopkeepers find that they benefit from students buying things from their shops. This is an advantage of being close to a school. The disadvantage is that the students all leave school at the same time, so it is difficult for other customers to get served if they shop at that time. The customers may decide to shop elsewhere. This is a disadvantage of being close to a school.

T A S K

The Table below shows a list of stakeholders. Choose TWO of the four businesses featured in the task above and complete the Table. You should write a short comment in each box explaining how the stakeholder is involved in the business.

Stakeholders	Business 1	Business 2	A real-life business located close to your school
Owners			
Employees			
Suppliers			
Neighbours			
Government			
Local community			

Organisation charts

An organisation chart is a diagram that shows how a business is structured. In a small business the chart may list employees by name, but in a large organisation job titles only might be listed.

Below is an example of an organisation chart.

T A S K

1 Choose a large department or faculty in your school. Draw an organisation chart using the names and job titles of the staff.

2 Draw an organisation chart of a Year Team or House from your school.

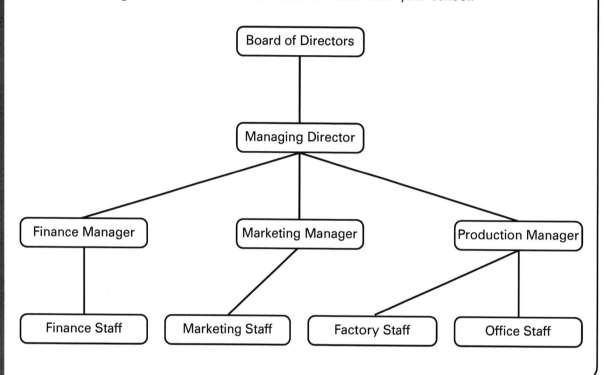

```
                      Board of Directors

                      Managing Director

   Finance Manager    Marketing Manager    Production Manager

   Finance Staff    Marketing Staff    Factory Staff    Office Staff
```

 Test yourself

1 Why should the owners of a new business decide on their aims and objectives?

2 Give an example of groups of stakeholders who have different viewpoints to each other.

3 How important is it to employ effective managers in a business?

Test yourself

1 How can staff influence a business?

2 What do trade unions do?

3 How can customer satisfaction be measured?

Test yourself

1 How can you decide whether a business is 'successful' or not?

2 Should staff be encouraged to join trade unions?

3 Discuss the key qualities of a good manager.

Crossword 1

T A S K

ACROSS
1 All businesses aim to increase these
3 Increasing this can be an aim of the business
4 This group of stakeholders rely on the business choosing them, and paying them for their own businesses to continue
5 This stakeholder can make laws that affect businesses
6 These stakeholders rely on the business for their income

DOWN
2 This organisation represents a group of stakeholders to the business's management
3 These stakeholders are responsible for ensuring the day to day running of the business

Wordsearch 1

N	O	I	T	C	A	F	S	I	T	A	S	R	E	M	O	T	S	U	C
F	F	A	T	S	O	T	T	V	N	N	O	O	N	M	T	R	T	K	M
R	U	D	S	E	M	I	A	S	O	I	A	O	A	S	T	A	N	I	I
E	P	B	J	T	S	N	A	I	N	U	I	R	F	T	H	D	E	O	C
A	A	A	N	S	C	A	T	Y	L	T	K	E	A	A	L	E	M	A	M
J	L	T	G	A	C	A	S	S	A	E	I	S	O	K	I	U	N	M	A
T	O	W	C	A	E	S	A	E	T	A	G	A	N	E	A	N	R	N	N
M	I	G	C	R	A	Y	R	S	S	N	R	I	G	H	T	I	E	L	A
O	I	D	C	R	A	C	H	O	A	I	K	I	S	O	G	O	V	A	G
S	R	B	I	O	H	A	E	H	E	M	B	S	K	L	I	N	O	A	E
C	O	N	S	T	R	A	I	N	T	S	O	I	D	D	A	S	G	N	R
J	T	T	L	E	E	A	A	O	E	O	L	S	O	E	R	T	V	I	S
R	C	A	Y	T	I	N	U	M	M	O	C	O	U	R	L	I	I	E	A
Y	E	N	O	I	T	A	S	I	N	A	G	R	O	S	R	U	V	O	S
W	A	I	M	S	A	T	O	V	D	I	T	S	A	O	I	I	R	A	N
P	R	O	F	I	T	A	B	I	L	I	T	Y	N	N	T	A	E	A	T
D	A	T	C	N	S	T	M	N	S	S	S	M	I	C	I	S	U	N	T
T	W	T	A	P	O	Y	S	O	S	A	E	N	E	C	A	O	C	C	O
I	C	I	S	S	O	U	T	D	A	N	T	J	I	T	M	G	S	B	Y
I	T	B	O	T	T	A	S	T	T	O	B	A	E	T	N	D	A	S	H
A	E	R	M	O	R	S	A	S	C	O	I	R	O	U	R	J	S	T	V

AIMS

COMMUNITY

CONSTRAINTS

CUSTOMERSATISFACTION

ENVIRONMENT

GOVERNMENT

JOBCREATION

LEGISLATION

MANAGERS

MARKETSHARE

OBJECTIVES

ORGANISATION

PROFITABILITY

STAFF

STAKEHOLDERS

TRADEUNIONS

WEALTHCREATION

Answers

Aims and objectives of business organisations

Task answers

Pendleton Pottery

Carrie should focus on maintaining a positive cash flow. None of her ideas for commissions will be successful if she has to close her business because she cannot pay for basics such as rent and clay.

Sewell Motors

Kier can focus on increasing his market share locally.

As the next-door property is already being used for car repairs he should have few problems adding it to his business.

Kier might also think about maintaining a positive cash flow in order to ensure that he can meet the extra costs of the new premises. This might be achieved by advertising his services more widely.

Theresa's Guest House

Theresa should concentrate on increasing her profit by ensuring that she is fully booked as often as possible. She might consider taking advance bookings so that she can plan ahead, and she should make sure that regular guests or firms who make frequent bookings know this. For example, she could tell the university accommodation office when she has spaces.

Perfect Private Tutors

The agency could focus on generating profits or (if there is another agency locally) increasing market share. It is likely that the teachers are employed on a casual basis, i.e. they are paid when they work and not when they don't. This means that the agency may not have to focus on maintaining a positive cash flow.

Organisation charts

Test yourself answers

1 *A business needs structure. It is wise to draw up a plan showing the owners' aims and goals for the business. Then the progress of the business can be monitored against the plan.*

2 *Employees hope to earn as much as possible. However, shareholders of a PLC or Ltd Company want a good return on their shareholding. The shareholders want costs – such as wages – to be as low as possible. This means the shareholders receive a bigger dividend.*

The local community want their area to be quiet and peaceful. They might object to late-night deliveries being made to a business in their area. However, the owners of the business might find that because the deliveries are made by lorry and the roads are quieter at night, this is the most efficient arrangement.

3 *A good manager will encourage the people that he/she is responsible for and make sure that they work as well as they can. A manager might have a qualification in Business Management and be up to date with the latest techniques for running an efficient firm (one where costs are as low as possible and revenue is as high as possible). If managers are poor and staff are unhappy, the staff will look for other jobs. Equally, there might be a high rate of absenteeism, where staff are absent for reasons that do not seem completely valid.*

Answers

1 If staff go on strike the business will not be able to run as it should. Staff who are very happy working for a firm will tell their friends and family how good their employer is, and the firm will build up a good reputation. When a vacancy is advertised the firm will find that many people apply, and they will be able to choose the best person for the job. Also, staff who are happy will stay in their job; it will not be necessary to keep training replacements for them, which is expensive.

2 Trade unions represent the interests of their members, give them advice and provide legal help if necessary. They also negotiate pay rises and adjustments to terms and conditions of employment.

3 Possibly by repeat business (customers who replace an item with another one from the same shop or manufacturer), or via questionnaires and feedback received at customer service desks/departments.

1 By comparing net profit year by year; looking at the market share held; checking the number of staff employed.

2 Every employee is entitled, by law, to join a trade union. If employees belong to a trade union it is beneficial because managers can negotiate with one person on behalf of the union members, rather than negotiating with all of the employees individually.

3 Able to lead, delegate, inspire staff, listen to staff, make decisions which can be justified, etc.

Answers

Crossword 1

```
              1P  R  O  F  I  T  S
              |              |2T|
              |              | R |
    3M  A  R  K  E  T  S  H  A  R  E
    | A |                   | D |
    | N |  4S  U  P  P  L  I  E  R  S
    | A |                   | U |
    5G  O  V  E  R  N  M  E  N  T
    | E |                   | I |
    | R |                   | O |
    6S  T  A  F  F          | N |
```

Answers

Wordsearch 1

```
N O I T C A F S I T A S R E M O T S U C
F F A T S O T T V N N O O N M T R T K M
R U D S E M I A S O I A O A S T A N I I
E P B J T S N A I N U I R F T H D E O C
A A A N S C A T Y L T K E A A L E M A M
J L T G A C A S S A E I S O K I U N M A
T O W C A E S A E T A G A N E A N R N N
M I G C R A Y R S S N R I G H T I E L A
O I D C R A C H O A I K I S O G O V A G
S R B I O H A E H E M B S K L I N O A E
C O N S T R A I N T S O I D D A S G N R
J T T L E A A O E O L S O E R T V I S S
R C A Y T I N U M M O C O U R L I E A
Y E N O I T A S I N A G R O S R U V O S
W A I M S A T O V D I T S A O I I R A N
P R O F I T A B I L I T Y N N T A E A T
D A T C N S T M N S S S M I C I S U N T
T W T A P O Y S O S A E N E C A O C C O
I C I S S O U T D A N T J I T M G S B Y
I T B O T T A S T O B A E T N D A S H
A E R M O R S A S C O I R O U R J S T V
```

The working environment

Cellular or open plan?

A cellular office is one where most people work in their own office or in an office with a small number of colleagues. An open-plan office is one where a large room is divided into sections, usually by low-level screens. Many people can work in the same open-plan office, and often they will be grouped in teams.

Modern offices tend to be open plan, although senior staff will usually have their own office. There are advantages with this system, for example it is easy for staff to communicate with others in their team. This system is cheaper for the business – less space is required as the staff work closer to each other than they would in cellular offices. Many businesses rent their office space and the price is worked according to square metres of floor space. Doors and corridors in cellular office arrangements take up a lot of space, which has to be paid for but cannot be used as a working area.

Open-plan offices have some disadvantages. Workers may find it difficult to discuss confidential topics and there tends to be constant noise. Other workers will be passing by on their way to photocopiers and printers, which is distracting.

TASK

1 Think of the offices used in your school. Sketch the layout of the school administration office, and compare it with a sketch of the Head Teacher's office. What differences do you see?

2 Find out what layout is used in at least TWO real-life offices. You might know about them from a part-time job, work that members of your family do, or from neighbours.

3 Think about the problems that workers encounter when working in open-plan offices. Write at least FIVE suggestions for a 'code of conduct' that could be used to improve their working conditions.

Test yourself

1 What are the advantages and disadvantages of an open-plan office?

2 If work done by employees is confidential, would you recommend an open-plan office or a cellular office?

3 Should managers have their own office, even though the employees they are responsible for are in an open-plan office?

Health and safety

Ergonomics

Ergonomics is the science of designing working environments so that people can work safely. It includes both the office itself and the equipment that workers use.

Repeating the same task over and over again can be harmful to a worker's health. Think about how you felt the last time you word processed a long piece of work or coursework. Now imagine that you have a job where you use a computer keyboard all day, five days a week.

ERGO-WHAT?

TASK

How can the computer equipment be modified so that it can safely be used all day? (Bear in mind that people come in all shapes and sizes.)

Think about the scenarios in the Table below. What should be done to protect the workers' health? Choose your solutions from the list below.

◆ Provide an adjustable footrest.

◆ Provide a mousemat with wrist support.

◆ Provide a keyboard wrist support.

◆ Provide adjustable chairs with good support for the back.

◆ Ensure that monitors can be adjusted.

◆ Provide training on adjusting equipment to suit individuals.

Scenario	Solution
New member of staff starts work and is shown to her desk	
Worker cannot reach the floor once the chair is raised	
Mouse must be used for design work that takes a long time to do	
Secretary is required to word process documents for most of the day	
Worker complains that uncomfortable chair is causing backache	
Worker comments that the monitor on his computer is difficult to see	

Health and safety

T A S K

In this illustration there are 10 health and safety problems – can you find them?

New working practices

Teleworking

Employees in some jobs can now 'telework', i.e. they work at home and keep in constant contact with their office by using a computer which is linked to their employer's network.

Teleworkers usually visit the office from time to time and a desk is available when they get there. This is where the expression 'hot desking' comes from – one desk is used by several people.

TASK

1 Complete the following Table.

Occupation or type of work	Suitable for teleworking? (Yes/No)	Reason
Firefighter		
Architect		
Teacher		
Taking orders from customers by phone		
999 operator		
Directory Enquiries operator		
Solicitor		

2 You are going to be interviewed by a national radio programme. They are running a feature on teleworking. Your employer is keen on teleworking and you have teleworked for two years. Here are the questions that you will be asked. How would you reply?

   a Why did you apply for teleworking when your employer offered it?

   b Do family and friends realise that they cannot disturb you when you are working?

   c Would you recommend teleworking?

Test yourself

1 Explain how 'hot desking' is linked to teleworking.

2 Why might some employees be keen to work from home?

3 When an employee is going to telework, a workstation will usually be provided by their employer for the teleworker to use at home. Why is this?

The importance of accuracy in preparation, storage and retrieval of information

1 Complete the text below by filling in the gaps using the following words:

Filing cabinets   Reference

Facts   Disk

Word processed   Alphabetical

There are many reasons why information must be prepared accurately. Financial data that is sent to the Inland Revenue must be correct, otherwise the firm could be fined. The text on packaging must be accurate, otherwise the law could be broken. _ _ _ _ _ quoted in advertising material must be true.

Copies of letters sent out to customers and suppliers must be kept. These used to be printed on paper and kept in _ _ _ _ _ _ _ _ _ _ _ _ _ _, but nowadays they are more likely to be _ _ _ _ _ _ _ _ _ _ _ _ on a computer and kept on _ _ _ _.

In order to find copies once they have been filed, a logical system must be used. All documents will have a _ _ _ _ _ _ _ _ _, which could be a number, date or name. It is common to file documents in _ _ _ _ _ _ _ _ _ _ _ order.

2 Information is likely to be stored on a computer. Give TWO examples of ways to prevent people looking at the information.

3 Suggest a method that a bank could use to file customers' correspondence and the bank's reply when the customers write or telephone the bank and the bank replies using word-processed letters.

4 What are the advantages and disadvantages of storing information on disk?

5 How does the Data Protection Act 1998 affect businesses?

Test yourself

1 What is a filing system?

2 Suggest a method of filing information so that it can be found again easily.

3 How can information be stored securely?

Effective use of resources

Resources are things that the business needs and they should be used carefully. Here are some examples of resources not being put to proper use.

> The lights were left on all night again!

> I don't know how he gets away with it – he is supposed to do the same work as me, but he gets through about half what I do each day and no-one notices.

> It seems a bit daft having four empty desks in here.

> This heating system is dreadful! On Monday it's always cold in here, and by Friday it is so hot I can't concentrate on my work.

> My computer broke down on Wednesday. It took until Friday afternoon to get it repaired and I am two days behind now.

TASK

How could the business solve these problems?

Effective use of resources

TASK

Look at the following illustrations. Which member of staff will work harder, and why?

> *Thank you for the report you gave me yesterday – I know you had to stay late to finish it. We got the contract.*

> *If you had done your job properly and sorted that report out, I wouldn't have looked so stupid in the meeting. You lost that contract for the firm!*

 Test yourself

1 Why should a business assess its office requirements regularly?

2 Why is it advantageous for businesses to train staff carefully?

Wordsearch 2

TASK

```
S Y E F F I C I E N C Y I E S T
E E T H O T D E S K I N G G E E
I R T E N A L P N E P O S N C E
T G G C F L B R R E D E E I U N
I O S G D A P S M A C E T L R Y
L N O C A O S P Y U G C G C E E
I O E C O E L D R C A O D Y U C
B M P S C O A I N R A E I C O C
I I C R Y R T W P A I R R E T C
S C R E N Y R G C S H L U R E S
N S R E I R N T A T E T E C Y L
O R G L C I I T A P G D L R C N
P G N I K R O W E L E T T A D A
S Y F R R N O I T A L S I G E L
E R O E G A R O T S O D R C R H
R W S H R E D D E D Y S L R Y P
W A S T A G E R E N G L H O N I
```

ACCURACY	LEGISLATION	SHREDDED
EFFICIENCY	OPENPLAN	STORAGE
EMPLOYER	RECYCLING	TELEWORKING
ERGONOMICS	RESPONSIBILITIES	WASTAGE
HEALTHANDSAFETY	SECURE	WORKINGPRACTICE
HOTDESKING	SECURITY	

 Test yourself

1 Who is covered by the Health and Safety at Work Act?

2 Workers who use VDU/computer screens are entitled to something under the Display Screen Equipment regulations. What is it?

3 When would basic health and safety instruction be given to a new member of staff?

Crossword 2

T A S K

```
        [1]       [2]
        [3]              [4]


    [5]



[6]




        [7]
```

ACROSS

3 A job that is carried out by a team of workers is likely to be done in this type of office (8)

5 The_ _ _ _ _ _ of a workstation should take into account the different heights of employees (6)

6 _ _ _ _ _ _ _ _ equipment is often used by people who work from home (8)

7 Confidential waste paper should be _ _ _ _ _ _ _ _ (8)

DOWN

1 Employees in certain jobs can be given the opportunity to work from this place (4)

2 Firms that use personal data must register with the Data Protection _ _ _ _ _ _ _ _ _ (9)

4 A secretary must ensure that all word processed documents are _ _ _ _ _ _ _ _ so that there is no misunderstanding later (8)

Crossword 3

T A S K

ACROSS

1 Office staff are often encouraged to _ _ _ _ _ _ _ paper (7)

8 The Display _ _ _ _ _ _ Equipment regulations refer to working with computers or VDUs (6)

9 Computer _ _ _ _ _ should be protected to prevent unauthorised use (5)

10 Businesses should find a safe way to _ _ _ _ _ documents so that they can be easily retrieved (5)

11 This type of office layout means people work in either their own office, or in one shared with very few other people (8)

12 This type of office layout is arranged in one large space (8)

DOWN

2 The study of office and furniture design to suit individuals (10)

3 This refers to people who work from home, then use a desk in the office when it is their turn to work from the office (10)

4 If a file is _ _ _ _ _ _ _ _ protected, then unauthorised people cannot read it (8)

5 The practice of working from home using a computer and modem to keep in touch with the office (11)

6 The Data _ _ _ _ _ _ _ _ _ _ Act states that data kept by a business must be accurate (10)

7 Many businesses now use _ _ _ _ _ _ _ _ packaging to show their commitment to the environment (8)

Answers

The working environment

Test yourself answers

1 Advantages include easier communication and less expense for the firm as equipment such as printers and faxes can be shared between several members of staff. Disadvantages include difficulty in concentrating on a complex task because of the constant noise, being able to hear other people's phone conversations, and lack of privacy.

2 A cellular office would be more appropriate. Examples of employees carrying out confidential tasks would be senior managers and secretarial staff working for them. Also, Human Resource managers dealing with confidential interviews would need somewhere to carry out those interviews.

3 Possibly – it depends on the tasks carried out by the manager. A junior manager, who combines the role of supervisor with managerial tasks, might be placed at a desk a little distance away from the team he or she is responsible for. A middle manager might share a cellular office with one or two other managers of the same status. A senior manager is likely to have a private office.

Health and safety

Task answers

◆ Frayed lead – possibility of electric shock.

◆ Old-fashioned fixed chair – no adjustment possible, likely to cause backache and other posture problems.

◆ Coffee mess – unhygienic. Used tea bags on floor are slippery – could cause a fall.

◆ Frayed carpet – easy to trip over.

◆ Tea spilling – could damage the computer and also cause electric shock.

◆ Filing drawer open – someone could walk into it and injure themselves.

◆ Handbag strap – possibility of someone tripping over.

◆ Peering at screen – employer should have arranged an eye test and spectacles.

◆ Rubbing eyes – should be allowed regular breaks from the screen.

◆ Carrying – unable to see where s/he is going, likely to trip. Also, could hurt back carrying heavy load.

Health and safety

Task answers

Essentially, the equipment needs to be adjustable. That includes the chair, table, monitor and keyboard. This will enable operators to set the equipment to suit themselves. A footrest should also be provided, along with wrist supports at the keyboard and on the mouse mat.

New working practices

Test yourself answers

1 For various reasons, teleworkers do travel to the office, e.g. to keep in touch with colleagues on a regular basis and to attend training sessions and meetings. Whilst in the office the teleworker needs a desk, so one is allocated to visiting teleworkers.

2 Common answers will include, 'So that they can look after their children'. It is important to understand that whilst teleworking makes dropping off and collecting school-age children easier, it is not compatible with full-time care of pre-school children. Answers could include people who would normally spend a significant proportion of their day travelling to and from work, and those who are fairly independent and suited to the self discipline required in order to work from home. Teleworkers need a space in their home to set up their work station and equipment, so they should have a home that is large enough.

3 Ergonomics and health and safety. Working on the dining table, lifting equipment into place every morning, will eventually result in injury. The employer will provide a suitable desk, etc., and the employee must use it.

Answers

New working practices

Task answers

Occupation or type of work	Suitable for teleworking?	Reason
Firefighter	No	Needs to be at the incident in order to deal with it.
Architect	Yes	Can use PC at home to draw plans and can communicate via email.
Teacher	No	Pupils need the teacher in the classroom with them.
Taking orders from customers by phone	Yes	Details can be entered onto a database, running on a PC linked to the office.
999 operator	Probably not	The nature of the work means the operator may need immediate advice and guidance from a superior.
Directory Enquiries operator	Yes	Can use database on computer provided by BT, no need to be at the office.
Solicitor	Partly	Could do paperwork at home and email it to the office. However, clients need to meet the solicitor face to face and these meetings are probably best carried out at the office.

The importance of accuracy in preparation, storage and retrieval of information

Task answers

2 Password on the computer itself, or the computer is stored in a secure room, perhaps with access via a swipecard.

3 A customer's bank account number is unique, so any filing system is more likely to use that number than the name of the account holder. The bank may have a hard copy of each letter in the file or, if it is a standard letter, a code relating to that letter may be recorded together with the date that it was sent. This information would also be held on the bank's computer system.

4 Disks are small and easy to store, but they can be damaged and then the data is not recoverable.

5 Businesses may only collect essential information from customers, and this will be stored on computer. The information should be updated regularly for as long as it is needed, then deleted when no longer required.

The importance of accuracy in preparation, storage and retrieval of information

Test yourself answers

1 It is a logical method of storing information so that it can be found again easily.

2 Alphabetically, by surname or customer name. Using a reference made up of the initials of the employee dealing with the customer and a unique reference number.

3 By using lockable filing cabinets, passwords and swipe cards for access to computers, and by restricting the number of staff able to access the information.

Answers

Effective use of resources

Task answers

1 *Ensure that a caretaker or cleaning supervisor checks that all lights are off once work has finished in the office. (These people usually work after the office staff have gone home.)*

2 *An appraisal system and formal method of checking what staff do will ensure that all staff work properly. In some organisations where computers are used, the key strokes of each member of staff are recorded, and this information is used to evaluate their work.*

3 *If the desks are to be empty for the foreseeable future, then the firm could consider moving to smaller premises which would be cheaper. Alternatively, staff could be moved into different offices or areas. If they have more space they may be better motivated and work harder.*

4 *The firm could consider an air conditioning system, or arrange for a visit from the heating engineers as soon as possible. It is expensive running big heating systems, and this one is clearly inefficient.*

5 *There should be a repair contract with a reliable firm that guarantees a fast service as part of the contract. Alternatively, a spare computer could be available whilst the repair is awaited.*

Effective use of resources

Task answers

The employee in the modern office has a more pleasant working environment. It has modern equipment and is light and airy.

The cramped office has little storage space and is unpleasant to work in.

It is likely that the employee in the modern office will feel more positive about his work, and will be better motivated.

Effective use of resources

Test yourself answers

1 *Office space is very expensive. If the business requires less space, then moving to a smaller office could be cost effective.*

2 *Well-trained staff will do their jobs well and with confidence. They are less likely to leave because they are under too much pressure. This means money spent on training is well spent. A high turnover of staff can prove costly.*

Effective use of resources

Test yourself answers

1 *Both employees and employers.*

2 *A regular eye test. If glasses are needed only to work with the screen, the employer must pay for them.*

3 *Probably during induction training as it would include information about fire drills as well as specific guidance for the workplace.*

Answers

Wordsearch 2

```
S Y E F F I C I E N C Y I E S T
E E T H O T D E S K I N G G E E
I R T E N A L P N E P O S N C E
T G G C F L B R R E D E E I U N
I O S G D A P S M A C E T L R Y
L N O C A O S P Y U G C G C E E
I O E C O E L D R C A O D Y U C
B M P S C O A I N R A E I C O C
I I C R Y R T W P A I R R E T C
S C R E N Y R G C S H L U R E S
N S R E I R N T A T E T E C Y L
O R G L C I I T A P G D L R C N
P G N I K R O W E L E T T A D A
S Y F R R N O I T A L S I G E L
E R O E G A R O T S O D R C R H
R W S H R E D D E D Y S L R Y P
W A S T A G E R E N G L H O N I
```

Answers

	¹H		²R					
	³O	P	E	N	P	L	⁴A	N
	M		G				C	
⁵D	E	S	I	G	N		C	
			S				U	
⁶C	O	M	P	U	T	E	R	
			R				A	
			A				T	
⁷S	H	R	E	D	D	E	D	

Task answers

Answers

Crossword 3

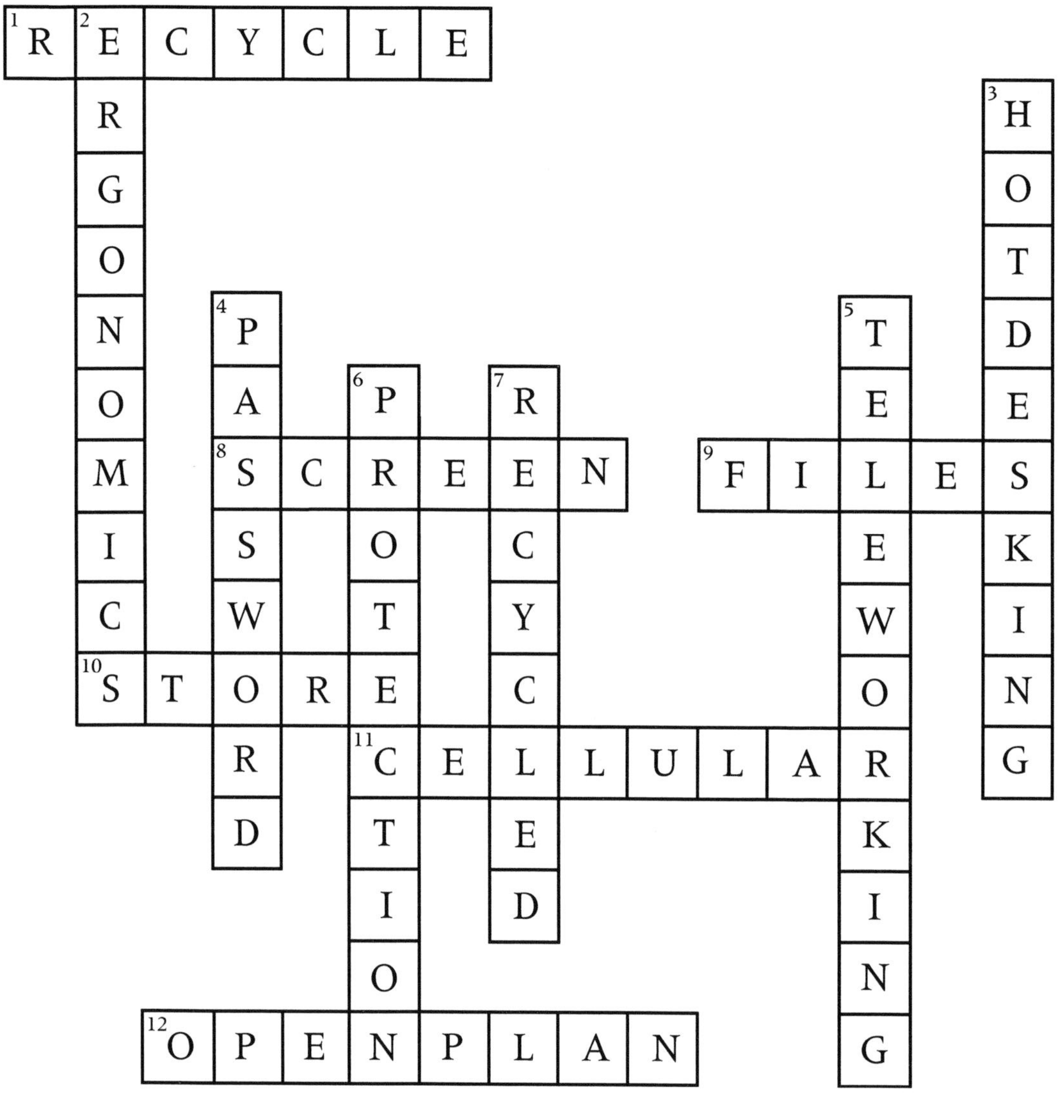
1 RECYCLE
2 ERGONOMIC
3 HOTDESKING
4 PASSWORD
5 TELEWORKING
6 PROTECTION
7 RECYCLED
8 SCREEN
9 FILES
10 STORE
11 CELLULAR
12 OPENPLAN

Task answers

Internal and external recruitment

There are many ways to recruit staff. The illustrations on this page show some of them. When choosing how to advertise a vacancy, firms must consider where the type of person they want to recruit would be looking for a job. The firm must also think about the cost of advertising the vacancy and they should choose the most appropriate method.

TASK

Where would you advertise these vacancies? (There can be more than one appropriate place.)

- Newspaper delivery boy or girl required.
- Office junior – suit 16-year-old school leaver.
- Graduate research scientist required for new project with major pharmaceutical firm.
- Hospital manager required – must have at least 10 years' experience. Very attractive remuneration package for successful candidate.
- Apprentice mechanic required.

- Part-time checkout operator required by large supermarket.
- Experienced sales representative required for engineering firm based in the North East. Excellent fringe benefits.
- Trainee bank clerk required.
- Experienced Personal Assistant required for Managing Director of animal feeds firm.

- Newly qualified secondary school teacher of Business Studies required.
- Motorcycle courier required – must have own bike and clean licence.
- Au pair required for family in London.
- Nanny required for family in Durham – two children under four years old.

- Practice Manager for busy doctors surgery in Nottingham.
- Apprenticeship in painting and decorating.
- Labourer for small building firm.

Senior Salesperson
PRESTO

Established company seeks an enthusiastic Senior salesperson to take on and grow the existing customer base.

You will have at least 5 years experience and a proven track record in sales.

You will be in charge of a small team of salespeople and will report directly to the Managing Director.

To apply, send your CV with expected salary to: Presto Products, HR Department, Presto

Test yourself

1 Give TWO examples of methods of internal recruitment of staff.

2 Give FOUR examples of methods of external recruitment of staff.

3 What is a CV?

Internal and external recruitment

T A S K

Matching exercise

List A should be given to students. List B must be cut up and students should then aim to match the correct word with the explanations in List A.

List A	List B
This organisation works with young people in school to help them find a good job with training	Careers service
It is possible to 'surf' this to find job adverts and information about firms before attending an interview	Internet
When all applications for a vacancy have been received, the decision must be made about which of the candidates to invite to interview	Shortlisting
In this type of interview there will be more than one interviewer	Panel interview
This training is given to new employees immediately they begin their new job	Induction training
Some large organisations will have their own training department and will run most courses themselves	In-house training
Most organisations send their employees to a specialist training firm to get a First Aid qualification	Off-the-job training
This method of pay means an employee is paid for spending a certain number of hours at work, i.e. 9am–5pm	Time rate
This method of pay means that an employee is paid according to how much is done, e.g. per carton packed, per shoe stitched	Piece rate
Some employees receive 'extras' such as a company car, a subsidised canteen or free work wear	Fringe benefits
This one-off payment is often made to employees at Christmas, or when profit figures are known	Bonus
Many people employed to sell things are paid a low regular salary and this is then topped up according to how much they have sold	Commission
This method of pay involves measuring what the employee has achieved over a period of time	Performance related pay
This pay is what the firm gives the employee before deductions of tax, national insurance etc.	Gross pay
This is the amount of pay the employee actually receives, i.e. after deductions	Net pay
This law states that employees who are doing the same job must be paid the same amount of money	Equal pay

Internal and external recruitment

TASK

List A	List B
This law states that employees must be treated fairly. It must not matter if the employee is male or female	Sex discrimination
Employees must be treated fairly, regardless of their colour or religion	Race relations
Employees must be treated fairly, regardless of their disability	Disability discrimination
Informing an employee that his or her job will no longer be available. This means that he or she has to leave the firm	Redundancy
An employee is able to draw a pension so decides to give up work	Retirement
An employee gives notice that he or she intends to leave the firm	Resignation
Telling an employee to leave immediately because he or she has done something seriously wrong (e.g. stealing, fighting)	Dismissal

TASK

Complete the paragraph by filling in the gaps.

Aftab received his _ _ _ _ _ _ _ on the last day of each month. The money was sent to his bank account. Aftab had recently received a pay rise, and was pleased to see that his _ _ _ pay had increased by £29.

He was quite worried about his job as three colleagues had been made _ _ _ _ _ _ _ _ _ . There was a lot of talk amongst the employees about more people having to leave. Aftab decided to update his _ _ in case he saw a good job that he wanted to apply for.

A job was advertised in the local _ _ _ _ _ _ _ _ _ . It asked interested applicants to telephone for an _ _ _ _ _ _ _ _ _ _ _ form. Aftab did so, completed the form and posted it to the business. A week later Aftab received a _ _ _ _ _ _ inviting him for interview. He got his _ _ _ _ dry cleaned and bought a new shirt. The interview went well and Aftab was offered the job.

Aftab's _ _ _ _ _ _ _ _ of employment required him to give one month's _ _ _ _ _ _ that he wished to leave. He wrote a letter to the personnel manager giving in his notice and started the new job five weeks later.

Internal and external recruitment

T A S K

1 Study the two cartoons. Why is the interviewee in the first cartoon more likely to get the job than the interviewee in the second cartoon?

2 Discuss with a classmate or your teacher what YOU would wear to an interview. State what type of job you would be interested in and sketch your interview outfit.

3 Think about the type of questions that an interviewer might ask. Write a script for a job interview, choosing a job that you would be interested in, showing how you would answer the questions.

 Test yourself

1 What is 'shortlisting'?

2 What is a panel interview?

3 How should an interviewee prepare for an important interview?

 Test yourself

1 What is a contract of employment?

2 Give THREE examples of information contained in a contract of employment.

3 What is a job description?

Remuneration

Payslip exercise

All employees must be given a payslip, whether they are paid weekly or monthly. Some employees who are paid wages (weekly pay) will receive their pay in cash. Most employees receive their wages in the form of a cheque or have them paid directly into their bank account. Employees who receive a salary (monthly pay) usually have this paid directly into their bank account.

> **T A S K**
>
> Why do you think firms prefer to pay wages and salaries directly into their employees' bank accounts rather than in cash?

Gross pay is the amount of money the employee has earned before deductions are made. ('Deductions' means money taken out of the gross pay.)

> **T A S K**
>
> The Table below lists some of the most common deductions. Write a brief explanation of each deduction.
>
> | Deduction | Explanation |
> |---|---|
> | Income tax | |
> | National Insurance | |
> | Union fees | |
> | Repayment of student loan | |
> | Pension contributions | |

Remuneration

Complete the following payslips. The first one is completed for you as an example.

Julia Khan earns £6.00 per hour. Last week she worked 40 hours.

Name	Julia Khan
Gross pay (£6.00 [x] 40)	240.00
Deductions	
Income tax (20%*)	48.00
National Insurance (9%)	21.60
Pension contribution (6%)	14.40
Union dues £3.00	3.00
Total deductions	87.00
Net pay	153.00

*Note: For simplicity, income tax is calculated at 20% in the example. Teachers should explain to students the income tax banding system.

Christina Short earns £5.00 an hour. Last week she worked 35 hours.

Name	
Gross pay	
Deductions	
Income tax	
National Insurance	
Pension contribution	
Union dues £1.20	
Total deductions	
Net pay	

Philip O'Donnell earns £4.50 an hour. Last week he worked 30 hours.

Name	
Gross pay	
Deductions	
Income tax	
National Insurance	
Pension contribution	
Union dues £0.75	
Total deductions	
Net pay	

T A S K

Remuneration

Type of pay	Explanation
Wages	
Salaries	
Time rate	
Piece rate	
Fringe benefits	
Gross pay	
Net pay	
Commission	
Overtime	
Bonuses	
Performance related pay	

 Test yourself

The employee and the workplace

1 Explain the term 'team working'.

2 Each employee expects to receive a payslip on a weekly or monthly basis. List FOUR items that must be included on the payslip.

3 How does a trade union assist with communication in the workplace?

4 What is an 'annual appraisal'?

5 Why is it important for a business that its employees are well motivated?

 Test yourself

1 Give an example of a law that affects business.

2 What does the Equal Opportunities legislation cover?

3 What changes to employment law have been introduced by the European Union?

4 How can employment be ended?

Crossword 4

ACROSS

1 A place where information can be displayed in a firm (11)

7 This may be provided in some workplaces (7)

9 Employees given a company car have to pay this on the vehicle (3)

10 Wages and salaries are examples of this (12)

13 A popular place to look for a job (9)

DOWN

2 Large firms may have their own _ _ _ _ _ _ _ _ department, providing courses for the staff (8)

3 Pay that reflects the amount sold by the employee (10)

4 Increasingly, male staff are allowed this leave when their spouse or partner has a baby (9)

5 Equal _ _ _ _ _ _ _ _ _ _ _ _ _ Legislation is the umbrella title for a range of laws relating to discrimination (13)

6 An interviewee should have prepared these before attending the interview (9)

8 Training that is run by the firm for its employees (7)

11 Female staff who have a baby are entitled to this type of leave (9)

12 An interviewee should be smartly _ _ _ _ _ _ _ for the interview (7)

Crossword 5

T
A
S
K

ACROSS

3 A list of your qualifications and personal details that you might send to an employer (2)

5 An employee who has reached the age at which he can _ _ _ _ _ _ can leave work receive a pension (6)

8 Employees must not be treated differently because of their _ _ _ _ _ _ (6)

9 Working extra hours for extra pay (8)

11 A place where jobs are advertised (9)

13 The amount of money actually received by the employee (3, 3)

14 An employee found to be stealing from the business will be _ _ _ _ _ _ _ _ _ (9)

DOWN

1 Training that takes place away from the workplace (3, 3, 3)

2 The name for the formal discussion with the employer, after which you may be offered the job (9)

3 The formal, legal document that sets out details of where you work, the hours, pay and holiday entitlement, which you must sign (8)

4 A company car, subsidised canteen and free uniform are all examples of these (6, 8)

6 Weekly pay (5)

7 The training that is done by a new member of staff (9)

10 Monthly pay (6)

12 A one-off payment for doing well at wok (5)

Answers

Internal and external recruitment

Task answers

◆ *Window of newsagent. School notice board.*

◆ *Careers Office. Local newspaper. Careers Co-ordinator of a Secondary School. Job Centre.*

◆ *Trade Journal.* New Scientist. *University Careers Office. National newspaper.*

◆ *Trade Journal. National newspaper.*

◆ *School notice board. Careers Office. School Careers Co-ordinator. College notice board. Job Centre.*

◆ *Word of mouth by existing checkout operators. School notice boards. Job Centre.*

◆ *Trade journal. National newspapers.*

◆ *Job Centre. School careers co-ordinator. Careers Office. Local newspaper.*

◆ *Local newspaper. Job Centre.*

◆ *Trade journal (TES). Local newspaper. Local universities' notice boards (education department).*

◆ *Job Centre. Local newspaper. Card in couriers' office window.*

◆ *The Lady. Au pair agency.*

◆ *Nanny agency. Trade journal. Local newspaper. Job Centre.*

◆ *Job Centre. Local newspaper.*

◆ *College notice boards and school notice boards. Careers Office. Local newspaper. Careers co-ordinators. Job Centre.*

◆ *Word of mouth. Job centre. Local newspaper.*

Internal and external recruitment

Test yourself answers

1 *Advertisement on a notice board, in a staff journal or by memo to branches/offices.*

2 *Job Centre. Advertisement in local or national newspaper. Advertisement in trade journal. Advertisement via recruitment agency or head hunter. Internet.*

3 *A curriculum vitae is a summary of someone's personal details, job and education history, and referees.*

Answers

Internal and external recruitment

Task answers

Aftab received his PAYSLIP on the last day of each month. The money was sent to his bank account. Aftab had recently received a pay rise, and was pleased to see that his NET pay had increased by £29.

He was quite worried about his job as three colleagues had been made REDUNDANT. There was a lot of talk amongst the employees about more people having to leave. Aftab decided to update his CV in case he saw a good job that he wanted to apply for.

A job was advertised in the local NEWSPAPER. It asked interested applicants to telephone for an APPLICATION form. Aftab did so, completed the form and posted it to the business. A week later Aftab received a LETTER inviting him for interview. He got his SUIT dry cleaned and bought a new shirt. The interview went well and Aftab was offered the job.

Aftab's CONTRACT of employment required him to give one month's NOTICE that he wished to leave. He wrote a letter to the personnel manager giving in his notice and started the new job five weeks later.

Internal and external recruitment

Test yourself answers

1. *The process of selecting which applicants to take up references for or invite to interview.*

2. *A panel interview is where there is more than one interviewer.*

3. *The interviewee should research the business, prepare questions to ask at the interview and dress appropriately for the interview. Appropriate dress will vary from a formal suit for an office or professional job, to tidy smart-casual clothes for a manual job.*

Internal and external recruitment

Test yourself answers

1. *A formal written agreement signed by the employer and employee. It sets out certain details of the job, disciplinary procedures and benefits.*

2. *Location of the employment, i.e. office address, branch address; remuneration; benefits/fringe benefits such as subsidised canteen, provision of work wear.*

3. *A job description gives details of the tasks to be carried out by the postholder.*

Answers

Remuneration

It is much safer than having a wages clerk travel to a bank to draw out the cash and then travel back to the office with it. Payments to bank accounts can be made electronically, and this is fast and straightforward.

Remuneration

Name	Christina Short
Gross pay	175
Deductions	
Income tax	35
National Insurance	15.75
Pension contributions	10.50
Union dues £1.20	1.20
Total deductions	62.45
Net pay	112.55

Name	Philip O'Donnell
Gross pay	135.00
Deductions	
Income tax	27.00
National Insurance	12.15
Pension contributions	8.10
Union dues £0.75	0.75
Total deductions	48.00
Net pay	87.00

Answers

Remuneration

Task answers

Deduction	Explanation
Income tax	Percentage of gross income paid to the Government
National Insurance	A percentage of gross income paid to the Government to fund a state pension
Union fees	Membership fees for a trade union
Repayment of student loan	Monthly repayment of loan taken out to complete a university course
Pension contributions	Regular payments that are invested to provide a pension when the employee retires

Remuneration

Test yourself answers

Type of pay	Explanation
Wages	Weekly pay
Salaries	Monthly pay
Time rate	Paid for working set hours
Piece rate	Paid according to how much work is done, usually in a manual job
Fringe benefits	Additional to pay – such as staff reduction on purchases, parking space, subsidies
Gross pay	Total amount earned before deductions
Net pay	Amount of take-home pay after deductions
Commission	Payment for making sales
Overtime	Extra pay for working extra hours
Bonuses	Payment for good work or because the business has done well
Performance related pay	Pay rises if targets are met

Answers

Remuneration

Test yourself answers

1 Employees work in small groups; sometimes these are permanent, sometimes they are formed especially to work on a particular project.

2 Gross pay. Net pay. Amount of deductions. Employee's name and reference number.

3 The trade union representative will negotiate with management on behalf of the staff in the union. Union representatives are usually trained by the union to do this effectively.

4 A discussion once a year between the employee and a manager, talking about the employee's performance and whether targets have been met. Recommendations for pay rises (or not) come out of these meetings.

5 Well-motivated staff will work hard when at work, and absenteeism will be low.

Remuneration

Test yourself answers

1 Health and Safety at Work Act 1974; Employment Rights Act 2002; Equal Pay Acts 1970 and 1983; Sex Discrimination Act 1975; Race Relations Act 1976; Disability Discrimination Act 1995.

2 Equal pay, sex discrimination, race relations, disability discrimination.

3 Working Week Directive, National Minimum Wage.

4 Dismissal, redundancy, retirement and resignation.

Answers

Crossword 4

```
      1N  O  2T  I  C  E  B  O  A  R  D
              R                          3C
   4P          A     5O     6Q           O
    A          I     P    7U  N  8I  F  O  R  M
   9T  A  X    N     P     E     N          M
    A          I     O     S     H          I
  10R  E 11M  U  N  E  R  A  T  I  O  N      S
    N     A        G     R     I     U       S
    I     T              T     O     S    12D   I
    T     E              U     N     E     R    O
    Y     R              N     S        R    N
          N              I              E
          I              T              S
          T           13N  E  W  S  P  A  P  E  R
          Y              S              D
```

Answers

Crossword 5

1 O		2 I		3 C	V									
F		N		O							4 F			
F		T		N			5 R	E	T	I	R	E		
T		E		T							I			
H		R		R			6 W				N			
E		V		A			A		7 I		G			
J		I		C			8 G	E	N	D	E	R		
9 O	V	E	R	T	I	M	E		D		B			
B		W					S		U		E			10 S
									C		N			A
			11 J	O	12 B	C	E	N	T	R	E			L
					O				I		F			A
					N				O		I			R
					U				13 N	E	T	P	A	Y
14 D	I	S	M	I	S	S	E	D			S			

Task answers

Methods of communication

There are many methods of communication available to both individuals and businesses. Increasingly, individuals take for granted communication technology that not so long ago would have been used solely by large businesses. Many homes now have a fax machine, often linked to a PC. Most young people have a mobile phone, and job application forms now invite applicants to give their email address as well as their home address. Interactive television is available to private homes; technology has come a long way since teletext services, which used to be the only information service available via television.

T A S K

Various methods of communication are listed below. Think about how they can be used by individuals and businesses. Discuss your ideas before completing the Table. (You might find it interesting to compare the attitudes of different generations, e.g. grandparents, parents and yourself.)

Method of communication	Use to an individual	Use to a business	Advantages of the method	Disadvantages of the method
Mobile telephone				
Pager				
Fax machine				
Teletext				
Interactive television				
Video conferencing				
Email				
Websites				

Methods of communication

T A S K

Method of communication	Use to an individual	Use to a business	Advantages of the method	Disadvantages of the method
Online banking				
Online shopping				
Bank Automated Clearing Service (BACS)				

 Test yourself

The effect of poor communication

1 What might be the consequence of an employee not understanding instructions?

2 Why do many businesses insist that staff taking customers' telephone calls use certain sentences? (e.g. My name is Andrew, how may I help you?)

3 Why is the 'grapevine' a potential problem for businesses?

 Test yourself

Formal and informal communication

1 There is usually a record of a formal method of communication, such as a letter or report. How might these records be stored securely?

2 List TWO advantages of presenting information in charts, graphs and diagrams.

3 List TWO advantages of presenting information in a report.

 Test yourself

Written communication

1 List THREE ways in which business letters differ from private letters.

2 Signs communicate information quickly. Sketch THREE examples of signs found in your school.

3 Sketch THREE logos. Do your classmates recognise them?

E-commerce

The internet has a variety of uses, from entertainment, help with homework and coursework, to an inexpensive way to communicate with family members living abroad.

Businesses also find the internet useful – a website allows potential customers to browse in their own time the products or services on offer. It is possible to place an order and make a payment via the website and to receive goods or services without meeting anyone from the business.

Email is a quick way of sending messages. It is much quicker than posting a letter and can be easier and cheaper than making a phone call.

A holiday can be booked using the internet without leaving home to visit a travel agent. The major supermarkets now offer a home shopping service, where groceries can be ordered at any time of the day or night, paid for online, and delivered during a time slot that suits the customer.

TASK

1 Discuss, either with someone in your class or with your family, the advantages and disadvantages of shopping using the internet. Draw a table to show the results of your discussion.

2 Would you recommend that a small speciality cheese shop has a website designed to advertise its cheeses?

3 Why might businesses arrange for their catalogues to be shown online?

4 Email is a very quick method of communication. What are the disadvantages of email?

5 Suggest at least TWO reasons why online travel agencies are successful.

Effective communication

T A S K

Fill in the spaces choosing words from the following Table. A word may be used more than once.

demotivated	misinformed	clients	formal	informal	discussion
meeting	video conference	telephoned	voicemail	letter	memo
fax	internet	email	website	online catalogue	booking service
report	message	notice	newsletter	mobile phone	pager

Raj and Amy were pleased to get jobs as trainees with Gilbert, Gilbert and Fish Solicitors. They were looking forward to dealing with enquiries from _ _ _ _ _ _ _. At the end of the first week Raj and Amy had a _ _ _ _ _ _ _ _ _ _ about what they had learnt.

Amy was surprised at just how many methods of _ _ _ _ _ _ and _ _ _ _ _ _ _ _ communication were used in the firm. Already she had been involved in a _ _ _ _ _ _ _ _ _ _ _ _ _ with the Huddersfield office. Once she had made detailed notes about the discussion, Amy had been asked to _ _ _ them to Huddersfield so that they could be checked.

When she did not hear by the next day, Amy _ _ _ _ _ _ _ _ _ _ the senior partner's secretary. The secretary did not answer the phone so Amy left a message on her _ _ _ _ _ _ _ _ _ service.

Raj, meanwhile, had been involved with a case where a client of Gilbert, Gilbert and Fish was claiming compensation for injuries received after slipping on a wet floor in a local supermarket. Raj found that Gilbert, Gilbert and Fish had been _ _ _ _ _ _ _ _ _ _ _ about the incident. Warning signs had been displayed to explain that the floor was wet.

Raj left a _ _ _ _ _ _ _ for Miss Gilbert on her _ _ _ _ _ _ _ _ _ _ _, and cancelled the _ _ _ _ _ _ _ arranged with the supermarket's manager. Raj then drafted a _ _ _ _ _ _ to the manager to explain the misunderstanding, and put a short _ _ _ _ on the file to explain what had happened.

Amy was interested to see a _ _ _ _ _ _ in the staff kitchen about a team-building weekend in the South West, that all staff were expected to attend, with an organisation called Morale Builders. There was more information in the staff _ _ _ _ _ _ _ _ _ _.

Raj suggested that they look up the organisation's _ _ _ _ _ _ _ on the _ _ _ _ _ _ _ _. He thought it might be a good idea to _ _ _ _ _ them for more information about suitable clothing for the weekend.

The _ _ _ _ _ reply from Morale Builders recommended waterproofs and strong boots. It also recommended a particular supplier. Fortunately, they had an _ _ _ _ _ _ _ _ _ _ _ _ _ _

Effective communication

TASK

so Amy and Raj were able to order what they needed in good time. Amy's boots did not fit properly, so she rang the _ _ _ _ _ number of the local representative of the supplier, who sent a replacement pair by courier.

After the weekend, Raj and Amy were asked to write a short _ _ _ _ _ _ for the Partners of Gilbert, Gilbert and Fish. However, it was difficult to hide how _ _ _ _ _ _ _ _ _ _ _ the staff were after their experiences.

As Amy remarked later to Raj, it was interesting to see how many of the colleagues were using the online _ _ _ _ _ _ _ _ _ _ _ _ _ _ _ of a travel agent to book a holiday so that they could recover!

Test yourself

External communications

1 Companies must, by law, publish their annual accounts. List THREE items that will be included in the annual accounts.

2 Communicating with suppliers is an example of external communication. How is this most likely to be carried out?

3 What regular communication would a business expect to receive from its bank each month or each week?

4 Market research is a communication method that allows the business to find out what its customers want. List THREE market research techniques that might be used.

5 Why do businesses provide an 'after-sales service'?

Communication

Communication role-play exercises

 Test yourself

Verbal communication

1 Suggest TWO reasons why formal meetings have a 'Chair' who controls the meeting.

2 Why are agendas and minutes of meetings filed and kept for some time after the meeting took place?

3 List TWO reasons why video conferencing might be used by a business.

4 What is 'voicemail' and why is it used?

 Test yourself

Written communication

1 What is the name of a written communication used within a business, i.e. from one employee to another?

2 This written communication is intended to encourage people to apply for a job with the business.

3 What is the name of an often detailed and long written communication used to put forward an idea or evaluate a project?

4 Which written communication tells an employee how much he or she has been paid for the month?

5 This is an important written communication used to confirm the job the employee has, and other details such as working hours and pay.

T A S K

The following exercises are intended for groups of four to six students.

Youth Club meeting

The local council are investigating setting up a new Youth Club in your area. In order to discover what local young people feel about the idea, your school has been asked to find out the views of a group of students in your year. The council have explained to your Head of Year that they need a formal record of what has been discussed and decided.

In your group, draw up an agenda for the meeting which should last 10 minutes.

Decide who will take which role during the meeting. Someone should be in charge of the meeting, and another person must take notes so that minutes can be produced. The rest of the group should decide how they will respond to the topics listed on the agenda.

After you have taken part in the meeting, each participant should have a copy of the agenda and the minutes. Individually write a formal letter to the council summarising your decisions. Explain that you have enclosed a copy of the agenda and minutes.

Suggestions for topics of discussion:

Days the club should be open	Code of conduct for club members
Possible locations for the club, based on the area you live in	Cost of membership and attendance
	Activities to be arranged
Times that the club should open	
	Adult staff required

Crossword 6

ACROSS

4   Good communication can help to
     _ _ _ _ _ _ _ _ staff (8)

6   A method of communicating information
     about products and services to the
     general public. Can be by television,
     or through newspapers (11)

8   Where voicemail messages are stored (7)

12   A formal written method of
     communicating a lot of information (6)

13   A formal annual interview where the
     employee and manager set targets for the
     coming year (9)

14   A formal written method of communicating
     with customers (6)

DOWN

1   A place in the workplace where
     information can be pinned up (11)

2   Getting together to talk about a problem (7)

3   A list of what will be discussed at
     a meeting (6)

5   A formal communication showing
     how much the employee has been paid (7)

7   Communication from outside
     the business (8)

8   An internal method of written
     communication (4)

9   Communication within the business (8)

10   A very informal verbal method of
     communication within businesses,
     that can cause problems (9)

11   Information needs to be _ _ _ _ _ _ _ _ so
     that mistakes are not made (2, 2, 4)

Crossword 7

ACROSS

3   A list of what will be discussed at a meeting (6)
4   A method of communication, popular with young people (6, 5)
5   This is shown on the internet to encourage people to buy from the business (6, 9)

DOWN

1   A popular method of communication used by schools to keep parents informed about events, results, etc (10)
2   Notes made about what was said in a meeting (7)
4   An internal written communication, used between people who work for the business (4)

Answers

Methods of communication

Method of communication	Use to an individual	Use to a business	Advantages of the method	Disadvantages of the method
Mobile telephone	Safety, convenience	Able to communicate with staff at all times	Becoming cheaper	Some areas still do not have mobile phone coverage
Pager	Can be quickly contacted	Able to attract member of staff's attention quickly and discreetly	Cheaper than a mobile phone	Need to find a phone to reply
Fax machine	Depends on whether s/he needs to communicate by fax. Quick and inexpensive way to send documents	Very useful for communicating where a paper record of a document is needed	Quick method of communication that cannot be 'hacked' into like a computer	Could be read by people who should not see the fax – usually staff do not have their own, personal fax machine. Cannot be accessed from outside the office
Teletext	Useful for checking share prices or last-minute holidays	Can check share prices	Easy access to television. Can look at teletext at home or at work	Being overtaken by the internet. Not interactive
Interactive television	Can be used to send email and make purchases	Possibly limited – a business is more likely to use the internet	Available to a wide range of people in their own homes	Tends to be slower than using the internet
Video conferencing	Unlikely to be used outside a business; individuals may prefer webcams	Very useful for a firm with branches in other countries. Body language can be assessed, which is helpful when a foreign language is being spoken	Much cheaper than sending staff abroad to meetings	Expensive to set up the system
Email	Easy, instant method of communicating	Individuals can access from their desks via passwords, thus ensuring privacy	Vulnerable to 'hackers'. Staff may use to send private messages	Cheap, fast method of communicating with others around the world
Websites	Many uses from shopping to information gathering	A tool for selling their product/service	Can attract clients who live at distance and would not normally consider using the firm	Need to be maintained, and for interactive websites security is important

Task answers

Answers

Task answers

Online banking	Very useful for those who are at work when banks are open	Banks can gain new customers and ensure satisfaction amongst existing ones who use the service	Provide most banking services (except cash withdrawal) over the internet 24 hours a day	For security reasons it takes time to set up. Some clients may not use this because of fears about 'hackers'
Online shopping	Very useful for people who work long hours, are housebound or have children and find shopping difficult	Supermarkets who offer the service will attract new customers	Home delivery at a time to suit the customer	Impulse buying does not happen as shoppers have to enter a list of what they want to buy, and they do not browse in the store
Bank Automated Clearing Service (BACS)	Salaries are generally paid by this method	Much more secure than paying by cash, which entails having to hold a lot of money on the premises on pay day	Fast, efficient money transfer service	Generally none

Methods of communication

Test yourself answers

1 Incorrect work. Possible injury of colleagues or customers; the business could then be faced with a large fine.

2 A standard greeting is part of the way that the business's ethos is communicated to the customer – polite and courteous staff will give the impression of good customer care and efficiency.

3 Rumours are often inaccurate and upsetting. The staff may be unsettled by an unfounded rumour that has escalated as it has spread, and the management may have no idea why consequently the staff are not working effectively.

Methods of communication

Test yourself answers

1 In locked filing cabinets for hard copies; on password-protected computers for computer files; or on floppy disk or CD.

2 If being presented to an audience, they are easier to understand than a complex speech or handout. Short and succinct.

3 Formal layout means that the reader can turn immediately to the sections relevant to them. Can be taken away and read at leisure.

Answers

Methods of communication

Test yourself answers

1 Business letters are written in formal English and do not make personal comments or indiscreet remarks.

E-commerce

Task answers

2 Yes, if it is able to produce enough cheese to fill all of the orders received. It should also consider how the cheese will be transported to the customer – is an expensive courier service required or can a cheaper, slower method be used?

3 This can attract customers who do not live near the showroom. If the website is also interactive, customers can place orders. This can increase revenue for the businesses.

4 It is vulnerable to hackers, and it is so fast that people might regret a reply that they send in the heat of the moment.

5 By cutting out the overheads incurred in running shops, the holidays can be offered more cheaply to customers, and the agency still makes profits. Also, the customer has access to the agency 24 hours a day, 7 days a week, unlike agencies based in the high street.

Effective communication

Test yourself answers

1 A balance sheet. A profit and loss statement. A message from the auditors that the accounts are accurate.

2 In writing, by fax or post, or via the internet.

3 A statement.

4 Telephone or postal surveys. Questionnaires. Analysis of sales figures.

5 After-sales service ensures that complaints reach the business so that they can be dealt with. It also means that properly qualified staff will carry out repairs, and customers do not have to arrange these themselves.

Answers

Communication role-play exercises

Test yourself answers

1 A Chair ensures that the meeting keeps to the allocated time. The Chair prevents the discussion becoming heated and personal. All items on the agenda will be brought up and discussed.

2 They are a record of the discussion that took place and they are vital in case the same topic arises again in the future or the actions taken after the meeting are challenged.

3 It is much cheaper than sending delegates abroad. Also, it helps to see the body language of the people being communicated with, particularly if they are communicating in a foreign language. These nuances would not be picked up via a telephone conference.

4 Voicemail is a telephone answering service run centrally by a business – instead of each employee having a separate answering machine on their desk, calls are recorded centrally on computer. Employees dial a special number in order to hear their messages, and it is possible to dial in from any phone (so calls can be checked from home).

Communication role-play exercises

Test yourself answers

1 A memo.

2 Job advertisement.

3 Report.

4 Payslip.

5 Contract of employment.

Answers

Crossword 6

				¹N							²M			
		³A		⁴M	O	T	I	V	A	T	E			
⁵P		G		O							E			
⁶A	D	V	E	R	T	I	S	I	N	G	T			
Y		N		C							I			
S		D		E		⁷E					N			
L		⁸M	A	⁹I	L	B	O	X		¹⁰G	G		¹¹U	
I		E		N		O		T		R			P	
P		M		T		A		E		A				
		O		E		R		¹²R	E	P	O	R	T	
				R		D		N		E		O		
				N				A		V		D		
¹³A	P	P	R	A	I	S	A	L		I		A		
				L						N		T		
								¹⁴L	E	T	T	E	R	

Task answers

Answers

Crossword 7

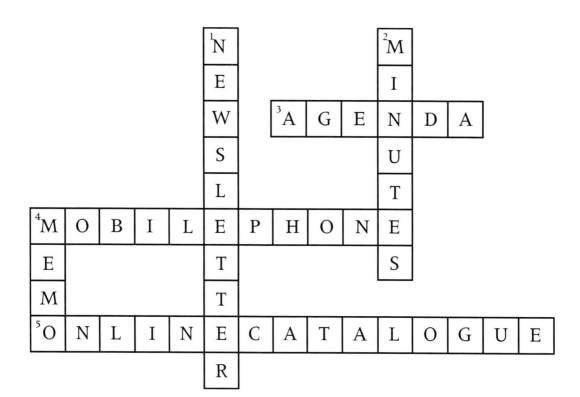

Task answers

Examples of common abbreviations

accom	accommodation	refd	referred
a/c(s)	account(s)	resp	responsible
ack	acknowledge	Rd	Road
advert(s)	advertisement(s)	Sat	Saturday
appt(s)	appointment(s)	sec(s)	secretary/ies
approx	approximately	sep	separate
Apr	April	Sept	September
attn	attention	sig(s)	signature(s)
Aug	August	sinc	sincerely
Ave	Avenue	St	Street
bel	believe	suff	sufficient
bus	business	Sun	Sunday
cat(s)	catalogue(s)	temp	temporary
cttee(s)	committee(s)	thro	through
co(s)	company/ies	Thurs	Thursday
Cres	Crescent	Tues	Tuesday
Dec	December	sh	shall
def	definitely	shd	should
dev	develop	Wed	Wednesday
Dr	Drive	wh	which
ex	exercise	wd	would
exp(s)	expense(s)	w	with
exp	experience	wl	will
Feb	February	yr(s)	year(s)
ffly	faithfully	yr(s)	your(s)
Fri	Friday		
gov(s)	government(s)		
gntee(s)	guarantee(s)		
immed	immediate/ly		
incon	inconvenient/ience		
Jan	January		
Jul	July		
Jun	June		
mfr(s)	manufacturer(s)		
misc	miscellaneous		
Mon	Monday		
necy	necessary		
Nov	November		
Oct	October		
opp(s)	opportunity/ies		
rec(s)	receipt(s)		
rec	receive		
recd	received		
recom	recommend		
ref(s)	reference(s)		

Word processing

T A S K

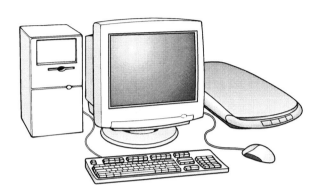

1 What are the THREE methods of inputting data onto this computer?

2 What methods of inputting commands can you see on this computer?

3 What methods of inputting commands can you see on this computer?

Word processing

Feature	Explanation
Underlining	Emphasising text by putting a line underneath it
	Emphasising text by showing it in a slanted form – rather like some handwriting
Centre	
Fully justified	
Right justified	
	A regular left margin and a ragged right margin
Mail merge	
	Amending the spelling of the same word throughout the text
Line spacing	
Tables and charts	

Presentation software

Visual aids for presentations can be created in a variety of ways. Powerpoint® is a well-known software programme which allows information to presented in a variety of ways. Transparencies can be created by printing onto acetates made for inkjet or laser printers; these are then used on an overhead projector.

TASK

Use the six slides below to draft slides for a presentation. Remember that these are your visual aids, not the whole presentation.

Spreadsheets

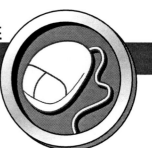

T A S K

Label the spreadsheet below with the following terms: cell, column, row, label, numbers, formula.

	July	August	September
Income from employment	552	432	442
Income from lodger	200	200	200
Total income	752	632	642
Expenditure			
Mortgage	280	280	280
Utilities	35	35	35
Community Charge	90	90	90
Total expenditure	405	405	405
Income minus expenditure	"=c7-C13	227	237

Charts can be drawn from data shown on a spreadsheet. Here are some examples.

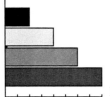 Bar chart
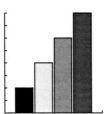 Column chart
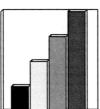 3D Column chart

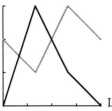 Line chart
 Pie chart

T A S K

You should always choose the most suitable chart to display data. How would you choose to display the following information?

1 Number of boys and girls in your Business and Communication Systems group.

2 Number of boys and girls in your school, and the year group that they are in.

3 Number of A*, A, B and C grades gained for Year 11 in your school. This is to be shown to parents on an overhead transparency during a talk by the Head.

Data processing

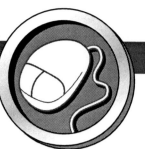

T A S K

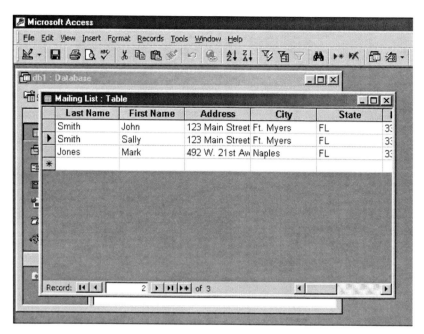

From the example above, write down:

1 TWO field titles.

2 TWO records.

T A S K

You have been asked to design a database to record information about students in your tutor group.

1 Give ONE example of fields that would have the following types of data in them:

  a text

  b numbers or numeric

  c alphanumeric

  d date.

2 Design a data capture sheet that could be used to collect the information you want for the database.

3 Why might you need to SORT the tutor-group data **numerically**?

4 Why might you need to SORT the tutor-group data **alphabetically**?

5 Give THREE examples of **queries** that you could use the tutor-group database to answer.

Graphics software

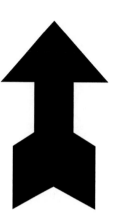

T A S K

Think of the work you have been doing on your course. Give at least one example of how you could make use of the following graphics functions.

1 Changing the shape of a block of text.

2 Changing the shape of an object you have imported into the work.

3 Changing the size of parts of a drawing.

4 Altering height or width of a drawing.

5 Rotating a drawing.

6 Cropping by deleting part of the drawing.

7 Changing the position of a drawing on the page, from top to bottom or right to left.

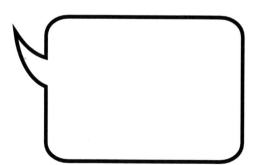

Desktop publishing software

Desktop publishing software allows text and graphics to be combined and laid out in a professional way.

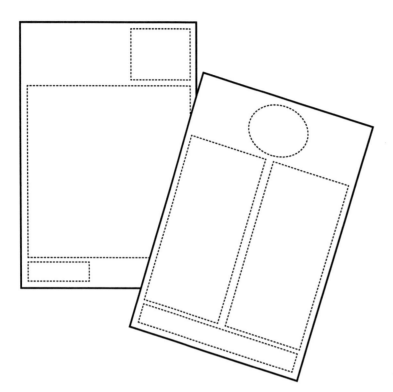

The DTP software will usually include a variety of suggested page layouts, for example for newsletters and leaflets.

TASK

1 Use a DTP package to create a tutor-group newsletter.

2 Explain what packages you could have used to create the newsletter if a DTP package was not available.

3 Compare the packages that you identified in 2 above (to produce a newsletter) with using a DTP package.

Test yourself

1 Give TWO examples of business documents commonly produced on computer.

2 Why might a slide show be created on computer by a business?

3 What type of documents is a business likely to produce using a desktop publishing package?

Test yourself

1 Give TWO examples of ways to input data onto a computer.

2 Give TWO examples of ways to input commands into a computer.

3 Give TWO examples of storage devices.

Crossword 8

T A S K

ACROSS

1 An alternative to a mouse or tracker ball on a laptop computer (8)

4 Using a database with a word processing package (9)

9 This is input to a spreadsheet to enable calculations to be made (7)

10 A device that allows documents to be copied onto the computer (7)

11 This looks like an upside-down mouse (11)

DOWN

2 Drawn from spreadsheet data (5)

3 A presentation package (10)

5 This field type is set up for addresses to be entered in a database (12)

6 A way of sorting information so that it goes from the lowest to the highest number or vice versa (11)

7 A 'box' on a spreadsheet (4)

8 A 'pointing device' on a computer (5)

Crossword 9

ACROSS

6 This is the name for a computer screen (7)

7 Paper that is printed in this way is shorter at the top than it is at the side (8)

9 One 'box' on the grid of a spreadsheet (4)

11 Making lists appear alphabetically (4)

12 This package allows you to add pictures and diagrams (8)

14 One computer amongst several on a network (8)

15 Taking a block of text from one part of a report and putting it in another part of the report (3, 3, 5)

DOWN

1 A page that is printed this way is wider at the top than it is at the sides (9)

2 This programme can carry out calculations (11)

3 An example of a pointing device (5)

4 A useful feature of wordprocessing programmes that makes sure all words are spelt correctly (10)

5 One piece of information held on a database (5)

8 This part of a database contains all the information about one person or item (6)

10 A disk with much more capacity than a floppy disk (8)

13 To line up text on a page (5)

Answers

Word processing

1 Keyboard, mouse, scanner.   **2** Keyboard, touch pad.   **3** Keyboard, tracker ball.

Word processing

Feature	Explanation
Underlining	Emphasising text by putting a line underneath it
Italicise or italics	Emphasising text by showing it in a slanted form – rather like some handwriting
Centre	Text is placed in the middle of the page with equal space to the left and right
Fully justified	Both the left and right margins are straight, i.e. each line of text finishes at the same set point
Right justified	A ragged left margin and a regular (or straight) right margin
Left justified	A regular (or straight) left margin and a ragged right margin
Mail merge	Link a database to a word-processing programme, in order to send standard letters that appear individual because each is tailored using the details of a firm or person on the database
Search and replace	Amending the spelling of the same word throughout the text
Line spacing	The amount of space between the lines in a word-processed document
Tables and charts	A method of displaying information in a document

Spreadsheets

COLUMN B   CELL C2   LABEL SHOWING MONTHS

	July	August	September
Income from employment	552	432	442
Income from lodger	200	200	200
Total income	752	632	642
		NUMBERS	
Expenditure			
Mortgage	280	280	280
Utilities	35	35	35
Community Charge	90	90	90
Total expenditure	405	405	405
Income minus expenditure	"=C7-C13	227	237

FORMULA
◄ROW 18►

Answers

Spreadsheets

Task answers

1 Bar chart or pie chart.

2 Bar chart. There is probably too much information for a pie chart.

3 Bar chart or pie chart.

Data processing

Task answers

1 The field titles are Last Name, First Name, Address, City and State.

2 A record is the information shown in the database, e.g. John Smith, 123 Main Street, FL.

Data processing

Task answers

1 a Name
b Age
c Address
d Date of birth.

3 To show age in ascending or descending order.

4 To create a set list.

5 Find all of the pupils with birthdays in a certain month. Find all of the pupils who live within walking distance of the school. Find all of the girls in the tutor group, or all of the boys.

Desktop publishing software

Test yourself answers

1 Reports, letters, memos, financial documents.

2 To show investors details of the business, to give information to staff, to present the results of an investigation to senior staff.

3 Leaflets, training documents.

Desktop publishing software

Test yourself answers

1 Keyboard, mouse, scanner.

2 Mouse, keyboard, tracker ball, touch pad.

3 Hard disk drive, floppy disk drive, CD drive, tape drive.

Answers

Crossword 8

```
        ¹T  O  U  ²C  H  ³P  A  D
                   H      O
                   A      W
  ⁴M ⁵A  I  L  M  E  R  G  E
     L           T      R      ⁶N      ⁷C
     P        ⁸M         R      U       E
     H           O    ⁹F  O  R  M  U  L  A
     A           U         I      E      L
     N        ¹⁰S  C  A  N  N  E  R      I
     U           E         T      R      C
     M                            I      A
     E                            C      L
  ¹¹T  R  A  C  K  E  R  B  A  L  L      L
     I                            L      Y
     C
```

Task answers

Answers

Crossword 9

										1 L				
		2 S								A			3 M	
4 S		P				5 F		6 M	O	N	I	T	O	R
7 P	O	R	T	8 R	A	I	T			D			U	
E		E		E		E				S			S	
L		A		9 C	E	L	L			C			E	
L		D		O		D				A		10 Z		
C		11 S	O	R	T		12 G	R	A	P	H	I	C	S
H		H		D						E		P		
E		E				13 A						D		
C		E				L						R		
K		14 T	E	R	M	I	N	A	L			I		
						G						V		
		15 C	U	T	A	N	D	P	A	S	T	E		

Task answers

Word processing

There are 10 spelling mistakes in the following memo. Correct them and suggest how Julian could avoid making them in the future.

MEMO

To   Phil Bennett

From   Julian Saunders

Date   10th June

Re   New pupil in Year 10

Phil, we've been asked to tak a knew pupil in September. His name is Adam Bolton and he has moved here from America with his family.

I have told Mr and Mrs Bolton that there son shouldn't have any problems keeping up with the rest of the group, as this is the first time they have studied Business. Adam has pickt this subject because he hopes to study Business at uneversity. Pearants work in the defends industry and are kean to help Adam settel in hear. They will stay for five years before returning to America.

TASK

The following information must be included in an advert for Cranberry & Brown, booksellers. Arrange it into a logical order, rephrasing if necessary. Add a border and graphics. Use a suitable font and font point size.

Opening hours – 9am–6pm Monday to Saturday, 9am–2pm Sunday

Large selection of books for children

Telephone 02011 483220

Story time 2pm–3pm in school holidays

20% off cookery books

email manager@cranberryandbrown.co.uk

27 Footes Walk, Newtown

TASK

This draft letter needs to be amended before it can be word processed and posted. Word process the final version.

Reference HC332

Dear Mrs Collins

Re: Your order of 12th November

Thank you for your telephone call this morning. I can confirm that your order was despatched yesterday afternoon.

I am sorry that you have had to wait so long for this order.

Yours faithfully   this does not reflect our usual standard of service

                          sincerely

Please accept the enclosed £30 gift voucher, to be redeemed against any item from our catalogue.

Mr I H Khan

Manager

Word processing

Methods of displaying text

Text can be displayed in a variety of ways. For example, in both books and newspapers the first line of each paragraph is *indented*. Advertisements are often *centred*. Reports can include *bullet points*.

T A S K

1 Explain what these methods of display mean.

Display method	Explanation
Blocked	
Indented	
Line spacing	
Centred	
Justification	
Enumeration	
Bullet points	

2 Identify each of these methods of display in the following text.

ANYTOWN PLAYERS

Anytown Players Amateur Dramatic Society requires new members.

Auditions will be held on 20th November in the Anytown Village Hall.

Prospective members should prepare to present:

1   a monologue lasting no longer than 10 minutes; OR

2   a poem of not more than one A4 page in length.

Also, each candidate will read the main character's part in a scene from a play, with members of the society taking the other parts. The play will be chosen by the society's director on the day of the auditions. Allowance will be made for candidates' unfamiliarity with the work if necessary.

Past performances include:

• As You Like It

• The Importance of Being Earnest

• The Caucasian Chalk Circle.

Word processing

Display features

Display features in text are ways of drawing the reader's attention to certain points. You have seen them used on exam papers, where the amount of time allowed and instructions about which questions to answer are **emboldened.** (This means that this section of text is darker than the rest of the text.)

T A S K

1 Explain what these display features are.

Display feature	Explanation
Closed capitals	
Spaced capitals	
Emboldening	
Italics	
Different fonts	
Font point sizes	

2 Now identify each of these display features in the following text.

A S N E W C O M P U T E R S

Cannon Lane

Midtown

MD3 4HN

As New Computers are pleased to announce that their HALF PRICE SALE will

continue next month. Included in the sale are Boyd ink cartridges, mouse mats

featuring cartoon characters, and ergonomic keyboards.

Telephone 02887 665 665 for more information or email

asnewcomputers@aaa.com

Word processing

Use cut, copy and paste functions

T A S K

1 Enter the following text.

HOUSE FOR SALE

27, Cambridge Walk is a spacious four-bedroom property. There is an en suite to the master bedroom, plus family bathroom with separate shower cubicle. There is also a cloakroom.

Downstairs there is a sitting room, dining room, study and a large kitchen/family room. The large garden is laid to lawn and there is a power point in the detached double garage. The central-heating boiler is located in the cloakroom. There is a range of fitted wardrobes in the master bedroom, along with a free-standing dressing table which is included in the sale.

The property is understood to be freehold. Offers are invited in excess of £220,000.

2 Move the sentence beginning 'The central heating boiler' so that it appears after the sentence 'There is also a cloakroom'.

3 The sentence beginning 'There is a range of fitted wardrobes' should appear after the sentence which ends with 'separate shower cubicle'.

T A S K

1 The layout of this invoice is unsuitable. It is difficult to read and to see how the final amount was calculated. Using an appropriate font and font size, set out the invoice so that it is easy to read.

2 How could the use of ICT help Mrs Clark in her gardening business?

3 Which programmes would you recommend that Mrs Clark learn to use?

From   Mrs B M Clark, Gardening Service, 12 The Lane, Anytown, Tel 07777 552 589
To   Mr and Mrs Evans, 187 Birch Avenue, Anytown.
Weekly mowing and gardening from 1st May to 31st August, £440. Petrol for lawnmower £12. Sharpening of hoe and fork £5.50. Total owed £457.50

Word processing

T A S K

Mrs Clark has asked for your help in producing some documents for her gardening business. The services she provides include:

- Regular mowing and weeding.
- Garden design.
- Advice on planting.
- Supply of plants.
- Setting up of vegetable gardens.
- Installation of ponds and water features.

1 Design a LEAFLET that can be delivered in the neighbourhoods where Mrs Clark would like to have more work. The leaflet should contain Mrs Clark's name, her address and phone number (see previous Task). It must explain the services she offers and ask prospective customers to telephone her for a free quote. Include borders and clip art. Choose an appropriate font and font size.

2 Design a BUSINESS CARD for Mrs Clark. This should just show her name, address and phone number.

Test yourself

1 What is a 'font'?

2 Why might you alter the spacing between the lines on a document?

3 What is the 'margin'?

4 Where would you see a 'footer' on a document?

5 Where would you see a 'header' on a document?

6 Why would you use the 'cut and paste' feature of a word-processing package?

7 How does a 'spell checker' help with word processing?

8 Why might the 'search and replace' feature on a word-processing package be helpful if you had spelt the name of a place wrongly throughout a document?

9 Why is mail merge used in offices?

10 What programme do you need in order to use mail merge (besides a word processor)?

Spreadsheets and charts

Open a new spreadsheet and enter the following information onto it.

Name	Race 1 position	Points	Race 2 position	Points	Total points
Max	5		5		
Philip	3		2		
Rajpreet	1		3		
Declan	6		7		
Stuart	7		4		
Alistair	4		1		
Francis	2		6		

1 Allocate points to the runners, so that first place = 7 points, and seventh place = 1 point.

2 Enter a formula in the 'Total points' cell to add up the points gained by each runner individually.

3 Insert two new columns, after 'Race 2 position' and before 'Total points'. These columns should be headed 'Race 3 position' and 'Points'. Enter the positions as follows:

Max	4
Philip	6
Rajpreet	2
Declan	1
Stuart	5
Alistair	3
Francis	7

4 Print a copy of the spreadsheet showing the formulae that have been input.

5 Save the spreadsheet.

Spreadsheets and charts

Open a new spreadsheet and enter the following information.

	May	June	July	August	September
Income					
Sales	2275.00	3792.30	5389.28	4229.40	3892.42
Rent of flat above shop	400	400	400	400	400
Total income					
Expenditure					
Materials	1884.20	1842.59	1957.66	2011.42	1953.25
Utilities	133	133	133	133	133
Insurance	80	80	80	80	80
Rates	150	150	150	150	150
Total expenditure					
Income less expenditure					

1 The spreadsheet shows income and expenditure for a small shop. Enter formulae to complete the calculations in the shaded cells.

2 Show all of the figures on the spreadsheet as currency.

3 Print a copy of the spreadsheet showing the formulae entered in order to complete the calculations.

4 Create a suitable, fully labelled chart to show the total expenditure of the business over the five months.

5 Save the spreadsheet and chart.

Spreadsheets and charts

A teacher keeps class results on a spreadsheet. Open a new spreadsheet and enter the following data.

	Test result out of 75	Homework result out of 55	Coursework result out of 75
Jane	36	12	54
Beth	21	25	37
Anne	47	30	55
Robin	8	51	52
Sally	62	39	60
Mike	44	42	46
Mel	18	50	42
Kate	32	55	59
Jeff	50	28	28

1 Convert all the scores to percentages.

2 Now sort the results and show the TEST results from highest to lowest along with the students' names.

3 Sort the results and show the HOMEWORK results from highest to lowest along with the students' names.

4 Sort the results and show the COURSEWORK results from highest to lowest along with the students' names.

5 Create a suitable, fully labelled chart to show the coursework results.

6 Save the spreadsheet and chart.

Open a new spreadsheet and enter the following information:

CAR BOOT SALE						
			Month			
	October	November	December	January	February	March
Number of cars	12	32	17	12	26	41
Fee per car	5	5	5	5	5	5
Total car receipts						
Rent payable for field	12	12	12	12	12	12
Amount received less rent payable for field						

Spreadsheets and charts

1 Ensure that the contents of all the cells can be seen fully.

2 Enter formulae to calculate the following:

　a the total amount received; and

　b how much has been received once the rent for the field has been deducted.

3 The owner of a hot-food van asks if he can park on the field during the boot sales. It is agreed that he will pay £50 each time he does this. Insert two rows between 'Total car receipts' and 'Rent payable for field'. Label one row 'Rent from food van' and the one below 'Total received'.

4 Input a formula in the 'Total received' row that will add the total paid by car owners to the amount paid by the food van owner.

5 Create a suitable, fully labelled chart to show the amount received less rent for field.

6 Save the spreadsheet and chart.

T A S K

1 Ensure that the contents of each cell can be seen in full.

Rainfall in cm	1999	2000	2001	2002
Weather station				
A	25.615	26.772	31.976	32.116
B	34.661	36.733	39.112	40.769
C	12.6	15.32	33.601	34.446
D	63.33	65.143	66.114	66.28
E	82.42	82.5	85.2	87.1

2 Format the cells so that the figures are shown to one decimal place.

3 Insert a column to the right of the column headed 2002. Label it 'Total rainfall'.

4 Input a formula in the final column to complete the calculations of total rainfall.

5 Create a suitable, fully labelled chart to show total rainfall.

6 Save the chart and spreadsheet.

CASE STUDY

The school visit

A weekend visit to Wilkins Hall Activity Centre is being planned for a group of 24 Year 10 students from your school.

1 There are five activities on offer: canoeing, caving, abseiling, high ropes and mountain biking.

2 Each student can choose to take part in three activities.

3 Health information must be collected from each student.

4 Parents' permission must be given in writing for each student to participate.

TASK

1 Design a data capture sheet that would be suitable to record this information on.

2 Set up the database using the following fields:
- Name
- Tutor group
- Age
- Saturday pm
- Sunday am
- Sunday pm
- Swimmer (yes/no)
- Health
- Permission received.

3 Use the following abbreviations:
- Canoeing – c
- Caving – cv
- Abseiling – a
- High ropes – hr
- Mountain biking – mb

and enter the following data.

Name	Tutor group	Age	Saturday pm	Sunday am	Sunday pm	Swimmer	Health	Permission received
Adam	10A	14	c	mb	a	no		Yes
Philip	10C	15	hr	mb	cv	yes	asthma	Yes
Ravinder	10C	14	mb	c	a	no	hay fever	Yes
Julia	10A	14	a	cv	c	no		Yes
Christine	10B	15	c	mb	a	yes		No
Harry	10A	15	hr	cv	mb	yes	asthma	Yes
Keith	10D	14	c	mb	a	yes		Yes
Aileen	10B	15	mb	cv	hr	yes		Yes
Anamieka	10C	14	a	cv	c	no		Yes

Databases

George	10B	14	a	cv	hr	yes		Yes
Bernie	10A	15	mb	hr	c	yes	asthma	Yes
Jeff	10C	14	c	cv	hr	yes		Yes
Ruth	10B	15	a	hr	cv	no		Yes
Rita	10D	14	c	a	cv	no		Yes
Lenka	10D	15	a	hr	mb	yes	hay fever	No
Sarita	10C	14	a	c	cv	yes		Yes
Robert	10A	15	c	cv	hr	yes	asthma	Yes
Rachel	10B	14	hr	c	a	yes		Yes
Anita	10C	14	a	c	mb	yes		Yes
Frederick	10A	15	mb	c	hr	yes	hay fever	Yes
Susan	10C	14	c	a	cv	yes	diabetes	Yes
Matthew	10D	14	mb	c	a	yes		Yes
Charles	10D	15	a	cv	mb	no		Yes
Stuart	10C	15	a	c	mb	no		Yes

Search your database to answer the following questions:

1 How many students are taking part in each activity on Saturday afternoon?

2 How many non-swimmers have opted for canoeing? Identify them and change their choice to mountain biking, as the instructor cannot take non-swimmers.

3 Which students have not returned their consent forms?

4 Sort the records so that the students' names appear in alphabetical order.

5 There is a problem with the high-ropes activity. List all the students who have opted for high ropes, so that they can be offered an alternative activity.

6 List all students who have asthma.

Databases

The Toy Factory

The owner of The Toy Factory (a toy manufacturer and supplier) has decided to keep customer details on a database. The database will also show which toys have been sent to the customers.

Set up the database using the following field titles:

◆ Name
◆ Address
◆ Contact name
◆ Telephone
◆ Fax
◆ Email

◆ Deluxe rocking horses
◆ Standard rocking horses
◆ Deluxe doll's house
◆ Standard doll's house
◆ Deluxe fort
◆ Standard fort.

Enter the following records.

Name	Address	Contact name	Tele-phone	Fax	Email	Deluxe rocking horse	Standard rocking horse	Deluxe doll's house	Standard doll's house	Deluxe fort	Standard fort
Cory Toys	3 East Parade, Anytown	Mrs Lynne Cory	02241 223812	02241 223813	Lcory@ corytoys. net	3	16		12	8	12
High Class Toys	58 Berry Arcade, Anytown	Anthony Sullivan	02241 233144	02241 211255	Sullivan @arcade. net				3		3
Bells Depart-ment Store	Tower St, Anytown	Mr H Singh	02241 442442	02241 442443	Personnel @Bells. com	6	3	15	21	8	4
Healey's Post Office	7 West St, Anytown	Mrs Zeynep Healey	02241 433212	02241 433516	Zhealey @info .net				2		
Save-pounds	186 High St, Anytown	The manager	02241 318324	02241 318612	Manager @save pounds .net				1		1

Databases

1 A field has been missed out. Enter this field, called STANDARD GARAGE. High Class Toys has been sent seven, and Savepounds has been sent one.

2 Search the records to find all businesses that have received the standard fort. Sort the results in descending order according to the number received.

3 Add the following new record: Brighter Toys, 12 Stanley Rd, Anytown. Contact Bill Brighter. Telephone 02241 545582, fax number 545522. No email details. Brighter Toys has been sent one standard rocking horse, and two standard doll's houses.

4 Produce mailing labels for the businesses on the database so that a mail shot can be carried out by The Toy Factory.

 Test yourself

1 Explain the difference between a field and a record.

2 Give at least THREE examples of uses of databases in business.

3 What is mail merge?

4 Why should care be taken in devising a data capture sheet to collect data that will be put onto a database?

5 Explain clearly how to carry out a search on the database programme you use.

6 Suggest how databases could be used in your school.

7 Give at least THREE examples of organisations where databases are used to answer queries or provide help.

8 Give TWO examples of numeric data.

9 Give TWO examples of alphanumeric data.

10 Give TWO examples of alphabetic data.

Graphics and clipart

A local primary school has asked for your help in designing a road safety leaflet for their 5–8-year-old pupils. The leaflet should be one side of A4, in simple language. There should be several illustrations. These can be from clipart or other imported pictures. The leaflet MUST include an example of freehand drawing and/or geometrical shapes.

Graphics and clipart

T
A
S
K

% %
% %

Write a brief report on your school's latest published exam results. The report should be in formal language and should include appropriate graphs to illustrate the points made.

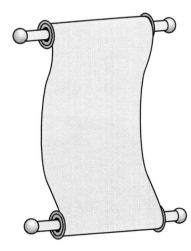

TASK

Write a short book for young children, where brief sections of text are supported by colourful pictures. Use a range of styles of writing in order to keep the child's attention. Use broken lines, repeat key words, and use an appropriate font and font size. The pictures can be from clipart, imported pictures or freehand drawings.

Answers

Word processing

MEMO

To   Phil Bennett

From   Julian Saunders

Date   10th June

Re   New pupil in Year 10

Phil, we've been asked to **tak** a **knew** pupil in September. His name is Adam Bolton and he has moved here from America with his family.

I have told Mr and Mrs Bolton that **there** son shouldn't have any problems keeping up with the rest of the group, as this is the first time they have studied Business. Adam has **pickt** this subject because he hopes to study Business at **uneversity**. **Pearants** work in the **defends** industry and are **kean** to help Adam **settel** in **hear**. They will stay for five years before returning to America.

The correct spellings are: take, new, their, picked, university, Parents, defence, keen, settle, here.

Errors can be avoided by using the spell-check facility and a dictionary for those words that sound right but are spelt wrongly. It is always a good idea to proofread work.

Word processing

Display method	Explanation
Blocked	Left and right margin are straight not ragged
Indented	The line starts part way across the page
Line spacing	The amount of space between lines in word processing
Centred	Text is equally spaced away from the left and right margin
Justification	Text follows a margin – e.g. 'right justified' means that text stops exactly at the right margin
Enumeration	Numbering points
Bullet points	Identifying points by using a marker, often a round symbol

ANYTOWN PLAYERS **Centred**

IndentedAnytown Players Amateur Dramatic Society requires new members. Auditions will be held on 20th November in the Anytown Village Hall. Prospective members should prepare to present: **This section shows left justification. Double line spacing shown throughout.**

Enumeration 1   a monologue lasting no longer than 10 minutes; OR

2   a poem of not more than one A4 page in length.

Also, each candidate will read the main character's part in a scene from a play, with members of the society taking the other parts. The play will be chosen by the society's director on the day of the auditions. Allowance will be made for candidates' unfamiliarity with the work if necessary. **This section is fully justified.**

Past performances include:

Bullet points •   As You Like It

•   The Importance of Being Earnest

•   The Caucasian Chalk Circle.

Task answers

Word processing

Display feature	Explanation
Closed capitals	Letters are shown in capitals, there is no space between the letters, e.g. CAPITAL
Spaced capitals	There is a space between each capital letter, e.g. C A P I T A L
Emboldening	A word or phrase is made to stand out by making it darker than the rest of the text
Italics	Letters slant to the right, rather like handwriting
Different fonts	Different styles of letter, e.g. Baskerville Old Face
Font point sizes	Different size letters, e.g. *22 point is this big*

A S N E W C O M P U T E R S spaced capitals
Cannon Lane **italics**
Midtown
MD3 4HN
emboldened As New Computers are pleased to announce that their **closed capitals**HALF PRICE SALE will continue next month. Included in the sale are **different fonts** Boyd ink cartridges, mouse mats featuring cartoon characters, and ergonomic keyboards.
example of different font and different font point size
Telephone 02887 665 665 for more information
or email asnewcomputers@aaa.com

Word processing

1 A style (i.e. shape) of text that the letters or words can be shown in.

2 To make it clearer to read.

3 The area of blank paper to the left, right, top and bottom of a page.

4 Within the bottom margin.

5 Within the top margin.

6 To rearrange the text so that it makes better sense.

7 It highlights words that are misspelt. (However, it does not highlight those words that are correctly spelt even though the meaning is wrong, e.g. their/there.)

8 You would only need to correct the spelling once, and the programme would make the change every time the place name appears.

9 To send standard letters that look personal.

10 A database.

Task answers

Test yourself answers

Answers

Spreadsheets and charts

	A	B	C	D	E	F	G	H
1	Name	Race 1 position	Points	Race 2 position	Points	Race 3 position	Points	Total Points
2	Max	5	3	5	3	4	4	10
3	Philip	3	5	2	6	6	2	13
4	Rajpreet	1	7	3	5	2	6	18
5	Declan	6	2	7	1	1	7	10
6	Stuart	7	1	4	4	5	3	8
7	Alistair	4	4	1	7	3	5	16
8	Francis	2	6	6	2	7	1	9

	A	B	C	D	E	F	G	H
1	Name	Race 1 position	Points	Race 2 position	Points	Race 3 position	Points	Total Points
2	Max	5	3	5	3	4	4	=C2+E2+G2
3	Philip	3	5	2	6	6	2	=C3+E3+G3
4	Rajpreet	1	7	3	5	2	6	=C4+E4+G4
5	Declan	6	2	7	1	1	7	=C5+E5+G5
6	Stuart	7	1	4	4	5	3	=C6+E6+G6
7	Alistair	4	4	1	7	3	5	=C7+E7+G7
8	Francis	2	6	6	2	7	1	=C8+E8+G8

Spreadsheets and charts

	A	B	C	D	E	F
1		May	June	July	August	September
2	Income					
3	Sales	£2,275.00	£3,792.30	£5,389.28	£4,229.40	£3,892.42
4	Rent of flat above shop	£ 400.00	£ 400.00	£ 400.00	£ 400.00	£ 400.00
5	Total income	£2,675.00	£4,192.30	£5,789.28	£4,629.40	£4,292.42
6	Expenditure					
7	Materials	£1,884.20	£1,842.59	£1,957.66	£2,011.42	£1,953.25
8	Utilities	£ 133.00	£ 133.00	£ 133.00	£ 133.00	£ 133.00
9	Insurance	£ 80.00	£ 80.00	£ 80.00	£ 80.00	£ 80.00
10	Rates	£ 150.00	£ 150.00	£ 150.00	£ 150.00	£ 150.00
11	Total expenditure	£2,247.20	£2,205.59	£2,320.66	£2,374.42	£2,316.25
12	Income less expenditure	£ 427.80	£1,986.71	£3,468.62	£2,254.98	£1,976.17

	A	B	C	D	E	F
1		May	June	July	August	September
2	Income					
3	Sales	2275	3792.3	5389.28	4229.40	3892.42
4	Rent of flat above shop	400	400	400	400	400
5	Total income	=SUM(B3:B4)	=SUM(C3:C4)	=SUM(D3:D4)	=SUM(E3:E4)	=SUM(F3:F4)
6	Expenditure					
7	Materials	1884.2	1842.59	1957.66	2011.42	1953.25
8	Utilities	133	133	133	133	133
9	Insurance	80	80	80	80	80
10	Rates	150	150	150	150	150
11	Total expenditure	=SUM(B7:B1)	=SUM(C7:C1)	=SUM(D7:D1)	=SUM(E7:E1)	=SUM(F7:F1)
12	Income less expenditure	=B8-B14	=C8-C14	=D8-D14	=E8-E14	=F8-F14

Task answers

Answers

Spreadsheets and charts

	A	B		C		D	
1		Test result /75	%	Homework result /55	%	Coursework result /75	%
2	Jane	36	48	12	22	54	72
3	Beth	21	28	25	45	37	49
4	Anne	47	63	30	55	55	73
5	Robin	8	11	51	93	52	69
6	Sally	62	83	39	71	60	80
7	Mike	44	59	42	76	46	61
8	Mel	18	24	50	91	42	56
9	Kate	32	43	55	100	59	79
10	Jeff	50	67	28	51	28	37

	A	B		C		D	
1		Test result /75	%	Homework result /55	%	Coursework result /75	%
2	Sally	62	83	39	71	60	80
3	Jeff	50	67	28	51	28	37
4	Anne	47	63	30	55	55	73
5	Mike	44	59	42	76	46	61
6	Jane	36	48	12	22	54	72
7	Kate	32	43	55	100	59	79
8	Beth	21	28	25	45	37	49
9	Mel	18	24	50	91	42	56
10	Robin	8	11	51	93	52	69

	A	B		C		D	
1		Test result /75	%	Homework result /55	%	Coursework result /75	%
2	Kate	32	43	55	100	59	79
3	Robin	8	11	51	93	52	69
4	Mel	18	24	50	91	42	56
5	Mike	44	59	42	76	46	61
6	Sally	62	83	39	71	60	80
7	Anne	47	63	30	55	55	73
8	Jeff	50	67	28	51	28	37
9	Beth	21	28	25	45	37	49
10	Jane	36	48	12	22	54	72

	A	B		C		D	
1		Test result /75	%	Homework result /55	%	Coursework result /75	%
2	Sally	62	83	39	71	60	80
3	Kate	32	43	55	100	59	79
4	Anne	47	63	30	55	55	73
5	Jane	36	48	12	22	54	72
6	Robin	8	11	51	93	52	69
7	Mike	44	59	42	76	46	61
8	Mel	18	24	50	91	42	56
9	Beth	21	28	25	45	37	49
10	Jeff	50	67	28	51	28	37

Task answers

Spreadsheets and charts

	A	B	C	D	E	F	G
1			Month				
2		October	November	December	January	February	March
3	Number of cars	12	32	17	12	26	41
4	Fee per car	5	5	5	5	5	5
5	Total car receipts	60	160	85	60	130	205
6							
7	Rent of field	12	12	12	12	12	12
8	Amount received less rent of field	48	148	73	48	118	193

	A	B	C	D	E	F	G
1			Month				
2		October	November	December	January	February	March
3	Number of cars	12	32	17	12	26	41
4	Fee per car	5	5	5	5	5	5
5	Total car receipts	60	160	85	60	130	205
6	Rent from food van	50	50	50	50	50	50
7	Total received	110	210	135	110	180	255
8	Rent of field	12	12	12	12	12	12
9	Amount received less rent of field	98	198	123	98	168	243

Spreadsheets and charts

	A	B	C	D	E	F
1	Rainfall in cm					
2	Weatherstation	1999	2000	2001	2002	Total rainfall
3	A	25.6	26.8	32.0	32.1	116.5
4	B	34.7	36.7	39.1	40.8	151.3
5	C	12.6	15.3	33.6	34.4	96.0
6	D	63.3	65.1	66.1	66.3	260.9
7	E	82.4	82.5	85.2	87.1	337.2

Databases

1 Canoeing: 7; caving: 0; abseiling: 9; high ropes: 3; mountain biking: 5.

2 Adam, Ravinder, Julia, Anamieka, Rita and Stuart cannot swim but opted for canoeing.

3 Christine and Lenka have not returned their consent forms.

4

Adam	Bernie	George
Aileen	Charles	Harry
Anamieka	Christine	Jeff
Anita	Frederick	Julia
Keith	Rachel	Ruth
Lenka	Ravinder	Sarita
Matthew	Rita	Stuart
Philip	Robert	Susan.

5 Aileen, Bernie, Frederick, George, Harry, Jeff, Lenka, Philip, Rachel, Robert, Ruth.

6 Bernie, Harry, Philip and Robert have asthma.

Databases

Task answers

	A	B	C	D	E	F	G	H	I	J	K	L	M
1	Name	Address	Contact name	Telephone	Fax	Email	Deluxe rocking horses	Standard rocking horses	Deluxe dolls house	Standard dolls house	Deluxe fort	Standard fort	Standard garage
2													
3	Cory Toys	3 East Parade, Anytown	Mrs Lynne Cory	02241	02241	Lcory@corytoys.net	3	16	0	12	8	12	0
4				223812	223812								
5	High Class Toys	58 Berry Arcade, Anytown	Anthony Sullivan	02241	02241	Sullivan@arcade.net	0	0	0	3	0	3	7
6				233144	233144								
7	Bells Department Store	Tower St, Anytown	Mr H Singh	02241 442442	02241 442442	Personnel@Bells.com	6	3	15	21	8	4	0
8													
9	Healey's Post Office	7 West St, Anytown	Mrs Zepnep Healey	02241 433212	02241 433212	Zhealey@info.net	0	0	0	2	0	0	0
10													
11	Savepounds	186 High St, Anytown	The Manager	02241 318324	02241 318324	Manager@savepounds.net	0	0	0	1	0	1	1
12													
13	Brighter Toys	12 Stanley Road, Anytown	Bill Brighter	02241 545582	02241 545582		0	1	0	2	0	0	0
14													

Databases

Databases

Test yourself answers

1 A field is a specific set of data, e.g. name or address. A record is all the data for one entry, e.g. Bill Smith, 12 Tanners Lane, Anytown.

2 BT uses databases for directory enquiries. Mailing lists are constructed using databases. Doctors store patient details on databases.

3 Mail merge is the linking of a database to a word-processing programme so that a standard letter appears to be written individually to all the people on the database.

4 The Data Protection Act states that only relevant information must be stored on computer, so the data capture sheet must not ask for any information that is unnecessary.

6 They could be used to store pupil details and to construct class lists.

7 BT (directory enquiries). Any organisation where stock levels are checked on a database before the customer pays, for example large department stores where the items on display are not always the ones taken away by the customer purchasing them (e.g. new furniture). Builders' merchants also store stock details on databases.

8 Date of birth; results in a test.

9 Address; National Insurance number.

10 Name; address; list of subjects studied.

Blythe and Sons

Blythe and Sons

Blythe and Sons is a dentistry partnership. The partners are Elias Blythe and his sons Adam and Christopher. The partners specialise in cosmetic dentistry, such as invisible braces, tooth whitening, caps and crowns. They are also a National Health dentist and have some vacancies for new patients. Their office is open from 8.30am to 6.00pm Monday to Friday, and in the second week of each month the office is open until 8pm on Tuesday and Thursday. These longer opening hours have proved very popular with their existing patients.

For some time now, Christopher Blythe has felt that the partnership would benefit from some local advertising, so he has been investigating the cost of this. He is concerned about the following article which appeared in the local newspaper.

DO WE NEGLECT OUR TEETH?

A local survey showed that people in the Northshire area are prepared to spend more on hair treatments, spectacles and clothes than on their teeth.
Why is this? Could it be that teeth are easy to forget?
Dentists recommend a check-up every six months. However, of 20 local residents surveyed, only seven had had a check up within the last six months.

1 Compose a formal letter from Christopher Blythe to Amanda Kennet, of Kennet Printers Ltd. Enquire about the cost of colour and black-and-white brochures advertising Blythe and Sons.

2 Compose two brochures for Blythe and Sons using different layouts and graphics in each one. Each brochure should have three columns. Write a formal letter from Amanda Kennet to Christopher Blythe pointing out the different features of each of the brochures.

3 Christopher contacted the local newspaper editor to say how concerned he was to read the article on local attitudes towards regular dental check-ups. The editor has asked Christopher to write an article on the importance of regular visits to the dentist. The article is not advertising for Blythe and Sons but a factual piece which must not be longer than 100 words. Compose the article.

4 Compose a memorandum from Christopher to Elias and Adam giving brief details of the article and the cost of advertising brochures.

5 Christopher decides to place an advertisement in the local newspaper for Blythe and Sons. The advertisement should include details of their opening hours and vacancies for new patients. Using an appropriate font and border, compose the advertisement, which must not be larger than a quarter of an A4 page.

Clegg and Sons Ltd, Estate Agents

CASE STUDY

Clegg and Sons Ltd, Estate Agents

A vacancy has arisen in our Anytown branch for a trainee. Initially the job will involve carrying out office based tasks. The opportunity may arise in the future for the suitable applicant to train as an Estate Agent.

You must be self motivated and able to work as a member of a team. A good telephone manner is essential. You must be prepared to work from Monday to Friday, 9am–5.30pm. One Saturday in four will be worked from 9am to 4pm. Time off in lieu will be given.

Please apply by letter, enclosing an up-to-date CV, to:

Mr G H Clegg, Clegg and Sons Ltd, 12 Garden Terrace, Anytown, AN5 2EE.

TASK

1 You have seen this advertisement in your local newspaper and have decided to apply for the job. Using the information in the advertisement, compose a formal covering letter to Mr Clegg and attach an up-to-date copy of your CV.

2 You were fortunate to get the job, despite 17 other applications. Well done! Now that you work for Clegg and Sons your ICT skills have been noticed. Mr Clegg is considering updating the appearance of the sale details produced by the office. At present, details are up to four pages long and they are monochrome. Mr Clegg thinks that shorter details will hold potential buyers' attention, and that colour should be used. Here are the details of a property just taken on by Clegg and Sons Ltd. Using this information, compose sale details of no more than two sides of A4. Include appropriate graphics, fonts and font sizes.

38 Mill Walk. Anytown. AN2 3YW. Price £87,900. Two bedroom Victorian terraced property. Sitting-room, 3m × 3.2m. Dining-room, 2.5m × 2.4m. Kitchen, 2m × 4.2m. Bedroom 1, 2.9m × 3.7m. Bedroom 2, 2.4m × 2.7m. Upstairs bathroom with shower over the bath. Small courtyard garden to rear of house. Original fireplace in sitting-room.

3 A staff training day has been arranged at a local hotel/conference centre. The day will include the following points:

a An update on the law relating to estate agency.

b Training on a new computer system.

c Discussion on streamlining office procedures.

d The conference centre has a restaurant, two bars, a conference room and lounge.

Using the details above, produce an information leaflet giving details of the venue and the training day. Use at least two columns and appropriate graphics, fonts and borders.

Magazine competition

Magazine competition

Your favourite magazine is running a competition. A poster is to be designed to encourage more people of your age to read the magazine. The poster should be on A4 paper and should incorporate graphics, clipart, borders and various fonts. It should be dramatic and exciting, clearly encouraging more young people to read the magazine.

CASE STUDY

TASK

1 Design a poster for the competition.

2 Write a short article for the magazine (no more than one page of A4 and in two columns). The article should be in the usual style of the magazine.

3 Compose a letter to the magazine commenting on an article you read recently.

The farm

The farm

A school governor visiting your class has mentioned her brother's farm. She explained that he has free-range eggs, home-reared lamb, and pick-your-own strawberries, peas and runner beans. Unfortunately, he is not getting the number of customers he needs to break even and he does not know how to reach new customers.

Your class have decided to help. The school governor has some ideas herself, and you decide to do the following:

1 Compose an advertisement for 'farm boxes' where a range of produce is delivered regularly to households in the local town. Each box will contain goods to the value of either £10, £20 or £30. The goods will vary according to the time of year. Box deliveries will take place on Friday each week. The advertisement will appear in the local newspaper and it will invite interested people to telephone for an order form which will be posted to them.

2 Design an order form. The form should also include a request for details of a safe place to leave the box if nobody is at home to receive it. The form should also state that payment by cash or cheque is required, and that if nobody is at home the payment should be made in advance by post or left outside for the delivery driver to collect.

3 Design an information leaflet which should include an order form. This will be left in various local shops that are keen to support the farm.

Style

1 How does a formal letter differ from a personal, informal letter?

2 What layout and style of writing should a leaflet have?

3 What is the purpose of adding graphics to a piece of writing?

4 How should a formal report be structured?

5 Sketch a suitable layout for a memo.

6 Sketch a suitable layout for a job advertisement.

7 What differences would there be between the language of an article for a young person's magazine and the language of a letter applying for a job?

8 What is a 'font'?

9 How can 'cut and paste' be useful in composing documents?

10 How can bold, underline and italic emphases be used in composing documents?

Answers

Style

1 A formal letter is usually word processed rather than hand written. The use of slang expressions will be avoided, and the letter will be laid out appropriately for a word-processed document. It will be polite rather than chatty.

2 Many styles could be suitable for a leaflet. In general, it should be clear and easy to read, and written in language suitable for the people that will read it.

3 Graphics help to explain and clarify the text.

4 It should be written in paragraphs, making use of headings, sub-headings and bullet points. The pages should have a header and footer, and be numbered. There should be a contents page, and there may be a bibliography and appendices if these are appropriate.

7 'Text message' English (the abbreviated language used on mobile phones, e.g. C U tonite) and exclamation marks should not appear in the letter, which should be written in a formal, polite manner.

8 A font is a style (i.e. shape) that letters appear in.

9 If a better order is seen for the paragraphs, they can be rearranged easily and quickly.

10 These draw the readers' attention to certain points or sections.

Test yourself answers

Advertisement

CASE STUDY

Haven Garden Centre

Haven Garden Centre is a family-run business. It was started by Alistair Haven in 1972, and although he is semi-retired he still has overall control. Alistair's daughter now runs the garden centre. Haven specialises in tropical and cold-water fish and has won prizes for breeding fish. There is a range of plants for sale including water plants for ponds. There is a car park for customers to use and a small café.

TASK

Advertisement

Set up a file on disk and call it ADVERTISEMENT. It should contain the following data. Set left and right margins at 3.17cm. Use a font size of 12 point and a ragged right margin.

The hyacinth bulbs are planted in terracotta pots which are imported from Italy. There are five bulbs in each pot, all of one colour. Colour choices are blue, red or white.

The pots are for sale at £19.99 each, and the bulbs will flower in early December.

Any customer purchasing more than one pot will receive a 10% discount.

Set up a file on disk and call it INSERT. It should contain the following data. Set left and right margins of 3.17cm. Use a font size of 12 point and justify the text.

Garden tokens are an ideal Christmas gift. They are available to the value of £1, £5, £10 and £20. Purchasers have a choice of free greetings cards in which to send the tokens.

Recall the file ADVERTISEMENT, which is the text of a flyer to be delivered via a free newspaper. Make the following amendments:

1 Merge the file INSERT into the document.

2 Cut and paste the paragraphs into a logical order.

3 Add a suitable title and give it emphasis.

4 Add one further piece of information from the scenario that you feel is necessary.

5 Use the facilities available on your computer, such as borders, clipart, fonts and styles to improve the appearance and impact of the flyer.

Save your flyer as FLYER and print.

1 Create a new file and use it to comment on the good and bad points of your flyer. Suggest improvements that you could make if you had more time.

2 Save this file as COMMENTS and print.

Database and memo

Database and memo

Set up a database on disk and call it CHRISTMAS ORDERS. Enter the following five field names and 10 records.

Surname	Forename	Address	Postcode	Order
Lucas	James	1 Tower Walk	BB2 5TL	Hyacinths
Goldsmith	Sara	15 Broad Rd	BB4 2HL	Hyacinths
Abbey	Son	89 Eve St	BB2 7BW	Door wreath
Farrington	Laura	The Rectory	BB8 4VL	Large tree
Pike	Eileen	3a Rose Walk	BB3 3NN	Hyacinths
Archer	Amy	6b Rose Walk	BB3 3NM	Small tree
Harding	Philip	55 The Avenue	BB8 9HC	Door wreath
Elliott	Jennifer	27 Eve St	BB2 6DF	Hyacinths
Haughton	Guy	11 Broad St	BB4 3HX	Small tree
Cooke	Brian	12 Eve St	BB2 8DF	Hyacinths

Set up a file on disk and call it MEMO. It should contain the following data. Set left and right margins at 3.17cm.

M E M O R A N D U M

TO

FROM

DATE

Recall the file called CHRISTMAS ORDERS, which is Haven Garden Centre's customer order database.

1 Search the database for all the customers who have ordered hyacinths.

2 Sort the records into alphabetical order by surname.

3 Print the selected records showing only the surname and address.

Recall the file MEMO and use it to compose a memo to Alistair Haven. Your memo must have a suitable heading.

In the memo, you should:

1 Explain how Alistair could use mail merge to send a personalised letter to each of the customers on the list.

2 Weigh up the advantages and disadvantages to Alistair of using a database to store customer information.

Save the memo as ADVICE and print a copy.

Letter

Set up a file on disk and call it LETTER. It should contain the following data (i.e. a letterhead for the garden centre). Set left and right margins of 3.17cm.

HAVEN GARDEN CENTRE LTD
The Square Begborough BB1 2GG

Alistair has received the following letter. He needs to think what to do to retain the customer's goodwill.

Jakob Carter
7 Fairlawn Rd
Begborough
BB4 5MM

Mr A Haven
Haven Garden Centre
The Square
Begborough
BB1 2GG   2nd October

Dear Mr Haven

I have just seen your Christmas flyer.

I would like to order a small Christmas tree from you, but I would like to know whether it will be from a forest where it will be replaced. Also, I'd like a bowl of hyacinths for my mother. Could I have a bowl of mixed colours instead of all the hyacinths being the same colour?

I have bought plants from you for the last 10 years. I have always been very pleased with the service I have received, and the quality of the plants.

Yours sincerely

Jakob Carter

Recall the file LETTER which is a letterhead. Use it to compose a reply on behalf of Alistair. Your letter should include the points listed below.

1 All of the Christmas trees have been bought from forests where saplings are planted to replace trees cut down.

2 The bowls are usually planted with one colour of hyacinths only. However, as Mr Carter is a good customer, a bowl will be planted with mixed colours.

3 Please send a deposit of £5 for the hyacinths.

Save your letter as CARTER and print a copy.

Tabulation

T
A
S
K

Tabulation

Set up a word-processing file on disk and call it WAGES. It should contain the following data. Set left and right margins of 3.17cm.

HAVEN GARDEN CENTRE

PART-TIME STAFF WAGES

Name	Month	Hours	Hourly rate	Gross pay (£)
Julian	November	42		
Malcolm	November	33		
Phoebe	November	14		
Alice	November	22		
Sally	November	15		

Recall the file called WAGES, which is a record of wages paid to the part-time staff. Each of the part-time staff is paid £5 per hour.

1 Add the hourly rate of £5 for each member of staff.

2 Calculate the pay due to each member of staff and enter this on the wages record.

3 Ensure that each column is correctly aligned.

Save the form and print a copy.

Spreadsheet

Teacher: Set up a spreadsheet file on disk and call it PURCHASES.
It should contain the following data.

	September	October	November	December
Hyacinth bulbs	600	550	200	150
Cost per bulb	20p	20p	20p	20p
Terracotta pots	70	50	25	10
Cost per pot	£4	£4	£4	£4

T A S K

Recall the file called PURCHASES, which is a spreadsheet. This shows the number of bulbs and pots purchased each month by Haven Garden Centre.

1 Enter a formula to calculate the cost of bulbs and the cost of pots.

2 Below 'cost' of the pots enter 'total cost'.

3 Enter a formula to add the cost of bulbs and the cost of pots for each of the four months.

Save the file as TOTAL COST and print one copy.

Answers

Spreadsheet

	A	B	C	D	E
1		September	October	November	December
2	Hyacinth bulbs	600	550	200	150
3	Cost per bulb	0.2	0.2	0.2	0.2
4					
5	Cost of hyacinths	=B2*B3	=C2*C3	=D2*D3	=E2*E3
6					
7	Terracotta pots	70	50	25	10
8	Cost per pot	4	4	4	4
9					
10	Cost of pots	=B7*B8	=C7*C8	=D7*D8	=E7*E8

	A	B	C	D	E
1		September	October	November	December
2	Hyacinth bulbs	600	550	200	150
3	Cost per bulb	£0.20	£0.20	£0.20	£0.20
4					
5	Cost of hyacinths	£120.00	£110.00	£40.00	£30.00
6					
7	Terracotta pots	70	50	25	10
8	Cost per pot	£4.00	£4.00	£4.00	£4.00
9					
10	Cost of pots	£280.00	£200.00	£100.00	£40.00

Task answers

British Waterways

British Waterways is a public corporation accountable to the Department for Environment, Food and Rural Affairs (DEFRA) in England and Wales and the Scottish Executive in Scotland.

It cares for a 2,000 mile network of historic canals and navigable rivers across the country and works to conserve the 200-year-old working heritage of the waterways, protect their animal and plant populations and provide a unique place for everyone to appreciate and enjoy.

As more of the canal network is restored and opened, the canals provide more recreational facilities. The British Waterways website gives information about helping with conservation as well as details on the closure of canals for repair.

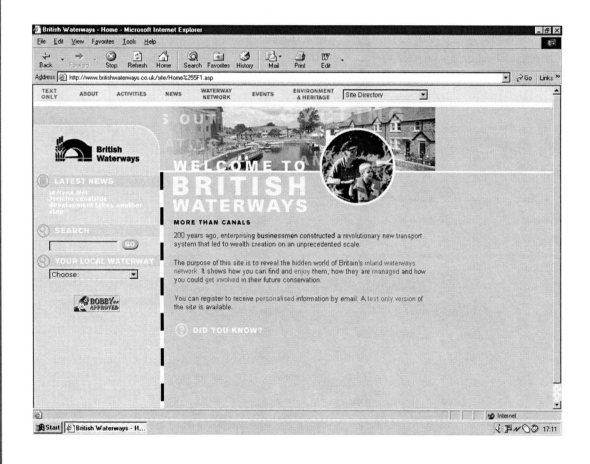

Test yourself

1 The website does not offer anything for sale. What is its purpose?

2 How could British Waterways use the website to attract more volunteers?

Hind and Hart Narrowboat Hotels

Hind and Hart Narrowboat Hotels is a private-sector organisation operating on the inland waterways of England. Each hotel boat (a narrow boat) has a crew of four as well as the guests. All the cooking and operating of locks is done by the crew.

The website emphasises the peace and tranquillity of the holidays. It is possible to view the programme and book online. Various journeys and places of interest along the way are listed and described.

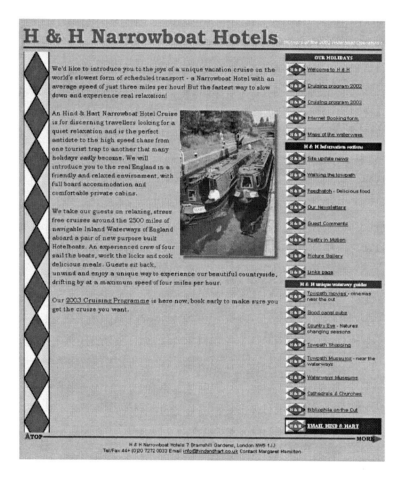

H & H Narrowboat Hotels

We'd like to introduce you to the joys of a unique vacation cruise on the world's slowest form of scheduled transport - a Narrowboat Hotel with an average speed of just three miles per hour! But the fastest way to slow down and experience real relaxation!

An Hind & Hart Narrowboat Hotel Cruise is for discerning travellers looking for a quiet relaxation and is the perfect antidote to the high speed chase from one tourist trap to another that many holidays sadly become. We will introduce you to the real England in a friendly and relaxed environment, with full board accommodation and comfortable private cabins.

We take our guests on relaxing, stress free cruises around the 2500 miles of navigable Inland Waterways of England aboard a pair of new purpose built Hotelboats. An experienced crew of four sail the boats, work the locks and cook delicious meals. Guests sit back, unwind and enjoy a unique way to experience our beautiful countryside, drifting by at a maximum speed of four miles per hour.

Our 2003 Cruising Programme is here now, book early to make sure you get the cruise you want.

OUR HOLIDAYS
- Welcome to H & H
- Cruising program 2002
- Cruising program 2003
- Internet Booking form
- Maps of the waterways

H & H Information sections
- Site update news
- Walking the towpath
- Feedwatch - Delicious food
- Our Newsletters
- Guest Comments
- Poetry in Motion
- Picture Gallery
- Links page

H & H unique waterway guides
- Towpath movies - cinemas near the cut
- Good canal pubs
- Country Eye - Natures changing seasons
- Towpath Shopping
- Towpath Museums - near the waterways
- Waterway Museums
- Cathedrals & Churches
- Bibliophile on the Cut

EMAIL HIND & HART

TOP

MORE

H & H Narrowboat Hotels 7 Bramshill Gardens, London NW5 1JJ
Tel/Fax 44+ (0)20 7272 0033 Email info@hindandhart.co.uk Contact Margaret Hamilton

Test yourself

1 What type of person are the holidays aimed at?

2 The website has links to other websites. What is the purpose of this?

Tesco.com

Tesco is a major supermarket. It is now possible to shop online with Tesco. The customer logs on to the website using a password. As well as grocery shopping it is possible to buy a wide range of goods. Job vacancies at Tesco are featured on the website as well as information about the location of stores.

Customers pay with credit or debit card. They choose a two-hour slot for delivery of their groceries which arrive in a temperature-regulated van. There is a freezer in every van so that frozen food does not defrost during the journey. The customer receives a list stating what was ordered and what is in the delivery. The driver of the van carries the groceries to the house.

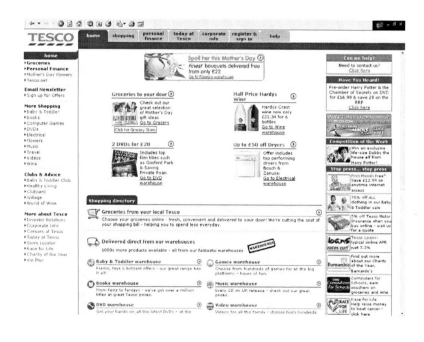

Test yourself

1 Home delivery is becoming popular. Why do you think this is?

2 Draft an advertisement to recruit home delivery drivers for Tesco. Include at least FOUR requirements relating to the attitude and experience of potential drivers.

3 Make a list of the types of people who would use this service and the types who would not.

Chelsea Building Society

CASE STUDY

Building societies have traditionally been based in high streets and shopping centres. The Chelsea Building Society's offices (known as branches) are open from 9am to 5pm Monday to Friday, and 9am to midday on Saturday. Most of the transactions on savings accounts are carried out either by phone or by post, or by customers visiting their local branch. However, application forms for these savings accounts can be downloaded from the website, which also features product and interest rate information. Some savings accounts have to be operated over the phone or by post. High rates of interest are available for these accounts.

Chelsea Building Society uses a website to advertise its savings accounts and mortgages. It also advertises vacancies at its Head Office in Cheltenham and in branches around the country.

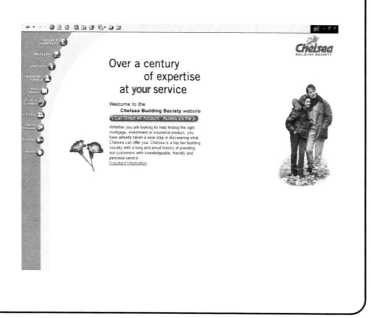

Test yourself

1 Give TWO reasons why Chelsea Building Society uses a website.

2 Why can investors prepared to use the internet, phone or post to operate their account get a high rate of interest?

3 Suggest TWO ways that Chelsea Building Society could persuade more customers to use its online service.

Premier au Pair Agency

CASE STUDY

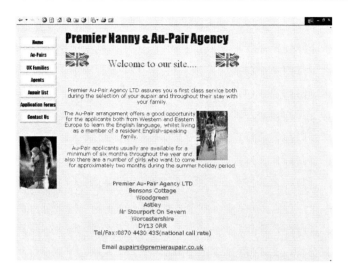

Andrea Payne had been running an au pair agency alongside her full-time job for some time. Six years ago she decided that to make the agency successful she would have to devote more time to it. Andrea resigned from her job and concentrated on expanding her au pair agency.

An au pair is a man or woman aged between 17 and 27, who comes to Britain to study English. He or she lives with a family and helps with housework and childcare in return for pocket money. The family helps to find an English course at college for the au pair to attend.

Andrea advertises her agency in 20 *Yellow Pages* and on the internet (www.premier aupair.co.uk). Sixty per cent of Andrea's clients see her advertisement in *Yellow Pages*, 30 per cent see the website and 10 per cent get to know about her via word of mouth. A disadvantage of featuring au pairs on the website is that more than one family might contact Andrea about the same au pair. Andrea set up the website in order to offer a better service to her clients. Families can see photographs of the au pairs and read about them online. The au pairs have to give permission for their

details to be put on the website. Not all au pairs agree to have their details shown.

Andrea finds au pairs for between 450 and 500 families each year. The busiest times of the year are July and August. Andrea cannot take holidays at that time because she is so busy. Families either want short-term au pairs (1–3 months) to help with the summer holiday, or are looking for a long-term au pair to start work with them (three months to two years).

Andrea has two employees. The employees need to understand the visa application process in the countries that they deal with. This is so that they can help the au pairs to get a visa. They must be polite and helpful on the phone to both foreign agencies and British clients. Andrea and her employees have good ICT skills. The information about the au pairs is scanned and put onto the website. Andrea estimates that this takes her about 10 minutes per au pair.

Clients pay Andrea by cheque or postal order for introducing them to their au pair. Andrea and her team make sure that the cheque has cleared before the au pair travels to Britain.

Premier au Pair Agency

Problems can occur once the au pair arrives in Britain. Some au pairs find that their English is not as good as they thought, and that they cannot understand the instructions they are given by the family. Andrea provides help and advice over the phone to families and au pairs who are having problems. However, most placements work very well. Andrea provides a great deal of guidance to families looking for their first au pair, and consequently she gains a lot of repeat business. (Families who have had one au pair from Premier au Pair stay with the agency when looking for subsequent au pairs.)

Test yourself

1 Why do you think the website is popular with Andrea's clients?

2 How could Andrea make more use of the internet?

3 Which computer programmes do you think Andrea is likely to use in running her agency?

4 Andrea and her employees work as a team. What are the advantages of working as a team?

5 Andrea has always used computers in her business. Do you think it would be possible to run this business without computers?

National Westminster Bank

C A S E   S T U D Y

National Westminster Bank (NatWest) can be seen on high streets and in shopping centres. However, it now operates a website, telephone banking for individuals, and a specialised telephone banking service for businesses. The business telephone banking service is based in Hornchurch, Essex. It operates from 8am to 10pm seven days a week.

It is possible to apply for a variety of services online, including savings accounts, loans and credit cards.

Test yourself

1 Branches of NatWest are usually open from 9am to 4pm or 5pm. Some are open on Saturday. Why do you think the hours for the business telephone banking are so different?

2 Evaluate the advantages and disadvantages to NatWest of running the business telephone banking service.

3 Evaluate the advantages and disadvantages to NatWest of operating online services.

Amazon

Amazon is a well-known seller of books, videos, CDs, etc. via the internet. It offers a secure payment system so that customers can pay by credit or debit card without worrying that hackers might get hold of their details. Purchases are delivered by post direct to customers' homes or workplaces. Customers find that when they log on to Amazon various products are recommended to them according to what they have bought before. These recommendations may include books by a particular author or music on a particular theme.

 Test yourself

1 What are the advantages to Amazon of trading online?

2 How do small bookshops continue to exist without selling online?

3 Why is Amazon able to offer reduced prices on its goods?

William Grey

William Grey is a family-run tool sales and hire business. It has a shop in Bristol which is open from Monday to Friday. The online catalogue allows customers to browse William Grey's stock and place orders. Some products are not available to buy online. Details of the products can be seen – links on the screen redirect the customer to other websites. A price can be discovered by telephoning the shop during opening hours.

Test yourself

1 The owners of William Grey operate one shop. Evaluate the usefulness of the online catalogue and website to the business.

2 What is the purpose of featuring links on the William Grey website to other web pages?

3 Would you recommend that small- to medium-sized businesses invest in a website?

Answers

British Waterways

Test yourself answers

1 The purpose of the website is to raise awareness of the activities of British Waterways. It also offers information to users of the canals.

2 Working holidays could be offered. The first page could have clearer links to volunteer opportunities. British Waterways could send information about volunteering and the website address to groups that might be interested, e.g. Duke of Edinburgh's Award groups, scouts, guides, etc.

Hind and Hart Narrowboat Hotels

Test yourself answers

1 The holidays are aimed at people who want a chance to experience travelling on the canal network without having to cope with opening lock gates, which is hard work. It is a quiet holiday.

2 Links allow potential customers to browse connected attractions; it might help to persuade them to choose the holiday if they can see an interesting package.

Tesco.com

Test yourself answers

1 More and more people work and an increasing number of households have access to the internet. Despite the longer opening hours of the supermarket, it is still time-consuming to travel to the store and shop. The delivery service appeals to a variety of customers.

2 Suggested requirements: clean driving licence; over 21 (for insurance purposes); able to deal politely with customers; able to lift and carry containers full of shopping.

3 Types who would use the service:

  a Parents who do not want to take their children to the supermarket.

  b People who dislike shopping.

  c People without a car.

  d People who have pets and do not want to carry bags of heavy pet food.

Types who would not use the service:

  a People without access to the internet.

  b People who enjoy looking for bargains/browsing at the supermarket.

  c People who live very close to the supermarket.

  d People who live in areas where the service is not offered.

Answers

Chelsea Building Society

1 A website allows Chelsea Building Society to reach existing and potential customers 24 hours a day. Nowadays, it is surprising to find that a well-established business does not have a website. Many people prefer to browse a website instead of making a journey to a branch.

2 It is cheaper for Chelsea Building Society to administer accounts run via the internet, phone or post. There is no need to maintain a branch, which will be in a prominent and therefore expensive position in a town or city. The high rate of interest encourages customers to choose this type of account.

3 Advertising could be carried out to draw the attention of potential customers to the website. Existing customers could be sent a mail shot with a special offer available if they move to the online service.

Premier au Pair Agency

1 People can browse in their own time. They can email Andrea when it is convenient for them. It is helpful to read about the au pairs and make an initial choice.

2 Possibly by enabling clients to pay online using credit cards. However, credit card firms charge a fee of about 4 per cent of the amount of the transaction.

3 Database for the au pairs' information and family information. Word processing for correspondence. Spreadsheet for accounts.

4 It might be possible for all members of the team to learn how to do each other's job. If one person is ill, the others can continue to do the work. Working as a team may encourage loyalty to the firm.

5 Yes, it would be possible. However, using the postal service as the main method of communication would be very slow. Making telephone calls to the agencies abroad would be very expensive compared to communicating by email.

National Westminster Bank

1 The business telephone banking is aimed at a different type of customer to those who operate personal accounts through branches. Many self-employed people work very long hours and cannot get to a branch. Being able to phone their bank manager until 10pm is an advantage to them in running their business.

2 Advantages include the possibility of attracting new customers. Disadvantages include having to either pay staff overtime to work until 10pm or have a shift system in place. This will need to be co-ordinated and extra jobs will be created in order to operate the service. This will be expensive, so the bank needs to attract sufficient extra customers to justify it.

3 Online services make the bank's services available to a wider variety of people. It will be expensive to set up initially, but the bank would hope that savings could be made elsewhere to justify the expense.

Answers

Amazon

1 *Online trading is cheaper than running shops and can attract a wider customer base.*

2 *They may specialise in particular types of books. Their customers may be people who prefer not to use the internet.*

3 *There are no overheads from operating shops and these savings can be passed on to customers.*

William Grey

1 *The online catalogue opens up their business to people who do not even know where William Grey is located. The cost of setting up the website should be covered by the additional sales generated.*

2 *It offers a complete service to customers – they do not have to carry out internet searches; the sites are easily accessible.*

3 *Possibly an advantage if they sell products that can be featured on the internet. Where services are offered the situation is more difficult – these are normally available within a radius of the firm's location.*

NOTES

NOTES

NOTES

NOTES